74-

One Man's Railway

J. E. P. Howey and The Romney, Hythe & Dymchurch Railway

J. B. Snell

DAVID & CHARLES

NEWTON ABBOT   LONDON   NORTH POMFRET (VT)

Contents

Acknowledgements	2
Introduction – The Place	3
1 Principals and Prehistory	5
2 Finding the Site	16
3 Equipment and Extension	23
4 The First Twelve Years	36
5 The War	49
6 Post-war Boom and Decline	53
7 Under New Managements	71
Appendix	88

Acknowledgements

Many people have given considerable help in the collection of material for this book, either by giving the author accounts based on their own memories of Howey, his family, and friends, or their personal experiences. No list could be complete, but major contributions were made by George Barlow, who has worked for the railway since 1947; Elenora Steel (née Greenly) and Ernest Steel, who have carried on her father Henry Greenly's model engineering business for many years; and Terence Holder, Manager of the RH&DR from 1946 to 1948 but involved with it since the visit of *Green Goddess* to Ravenglass in 1925. Other important contributions were made in particular areas by 'Jumbo' Goddard, R. M. Tyrrell, Col. K. Cantlie, Hugh Tours for much motoring detail, and David Laing, whose researches for the RH&DR's Golden Jubilee Exhibition unearthed much useful early information, including the Russian Connection. Valuable advice was given on other matters at typescript stage by W. J. K. Davies, and extremely efficient extraction work from various archives performed by the Imperial War Museum and the National Motor Museum at Beaulieu.

Most of all, however, is due to the many people, including those already named but also many others, who have over the years spoken with the author and told him their own stories, often over many meetings. Peter Hawkins was perhaps the most informative, having had the interesting experience of being pitchforked into the Manager's office not knowing a smokebox from a firebox (in his own words) and running the railway successfully through times as difficult as any before or since. But the author must record his obligation to many more.

It is impossible to name them all, but they include many employees and ex-employees. The RH&DR has certainly exerted a powerful spell on a lot of people, and exacted a degree of loyalty and devotion quite unusual even in these minor railway undertakings. One cannot spend any time at New Romney without being made strongly aware of this. So perhaps the final acknowledgement should go to the hundreds – or thousands – of people who over the years have all helped to make it live.

British Library Cataloguing in Publication Data

Snell, J. B.
    One man's railway.
    1. Romney, Hythe and Dymchurch Railway –
    History   2. Romney, Hythe and Dymchurch
    Light Railway – History
    I. Title
    385'.52'09422395   HE3821.R/

ISBN 0-7153-8325-6

© J. B. Snell 1983

Title page:
Howey and Greenly contemplating *The Bug* shortly after its delivery to New Romney in 1926. In the background, *Red Tiles* is under construction. *(E. A. Spring)*

Photoset by
Northern Phototypesetting Co. Bolton
and printed in Great Britain by
Biddles Ltd, Guildford, Surrey
for David & Charles (Publishers) Limited
Brunel House   Newton Abbot   Devon

Published in the United States of America
by David & Charles Inc
North Pomfret   Vermont 05053   USA

Introduction
The Place

It is no use pretending that the natural beauties of the South-East coastline of England have been much enhanced by human activity during the last hundred years. All the way round from Essex to Dorset, the generally rather reticent original charm of the landscape has been obliterated within a mile or so of the beach beneath a crust of bricks and concrete. There are of course factories and docks and power stations, but the greatest expanse is of small houses, each representing the modest fulfilment of dreams of retirement by the sea. Here and there along the two hundred mile sweep there are some gaps; the lines of great cliffs at Dover, Beachy Head, and Purbeck stand high beyond any spoilation, and occasionally, as in the Cuckmere Valley, there is a length which was never built over thanks to the obstinacy and sentimental unrealism of some very rich and long-lived families of landowners, not all of whom lived to see much appreciation of their stand. But, with the further exception of the centres of a few of the old small towns, very little else is unchanged.

The generally rather reticent original charm of the landscape . . . what kind of description should these words convey? In fact a great deal of it remains. For the remarkable thing about the coastal blight is that it is such a thin skin. Inland, plenty is left. Many landmark towns are listed in the guidebooks, and several writers have caught the soul of this part of England. Kipling, of course, pinned down the *genius loci* of every place he knew, even though by the time he came to live in Sussex development was spreading at its fastest. As he said, it is a land which has known great wealth; timber and iron, and earlier and later than those, wool and ships. It lost the industry a long time ago to distant parts of the kingdom, so long ago indeed that most children are taught that British ironmaking began in Shropshire and South Wales. Its people, too, are reticent, speaking seldom of these things and never to complain of them. Its ancient wealth has left many lovely buildings, and its farms still prosper. The pressure of twentieth-century change, urban growth and a rising population, could perhaps sweep away and destroy all this, but has not done so yet; and while it all remains, it remains itself.

Romney Marsh lies at the heart of this land; a level triangle edged on the north by the line of the Dover cliffs. After Folkestone, these leave the sea and march inland, gradually dwindling to low hills and the Wealden plains. On the west the Marsh is bounded by the line of the River Rother, and the hills of Sussex which climb towards the coast to become the cliffs at Fairlight, between Winchelsea and Hastings. To the south and east lies the sea. 'Marsh' has not, these thousand years, been an accurate word to use. The sea has been kept out by walls, some of which date back to the time of the Romans, and with the salt gone the soil is very fertile. But the retreat of the sea has not been due only to man's efforts. In remoter geological times the land area of the Marsh has risen above and fallen below the level of the sea at least twice, and over the last two thousand years it has tended to rise. Over the same period, the action of the tides and the prevailing winds has been to eat away at the soft, gravelly cliffs to the west, and to roll the shingle flints (which were all that remained after they fell) steadily eastwards along the sea bed until they reached deep water. In this way a bar or spit has grown across each river mouth, and most noticeably the headland at Dungeness has been steadily built up, a process which continues at the rate of several yards a year at the tip of the point. Much of the southern part of Romney Marsh is thus protected from the sea by this large area of relatively recent shingle-land.

In Roman times the Dungeness area was effectively an island, stony and infertile, and most of the Marsh really was a marsh. Three rivers, Brede, Tillingham, and Rother (once Limene) flowed out of the hills and into it before they reached the sea. The main flow of the Limene was then due east, meeting the coast where Hythe now stands, and its estuary made an excellent harbour. Here stood one of the main Roman narrow-seas ports, and some of the ruins of the town and fortress of Portus Lemanis still stand below today's Lympne (pronounced Limm) Castle. Later called Stutfall Castle, these stones mark one of the nine Forts of the Saxon Shore which defended Britain under the Romans and after.

But Port Lympne was already, even then, silting up and becoming unusable. This was partly because its mouth was barred by a growing shingle drift, and partly because the northern part of the Marsh had been enclosed by the Rhee Wall, which ran from Appledore to Romney, and claimed for cultivation. This diverted the Rother to reach the sea through Romney Haven, another large, shallow, sheltered anchorage. Gradually Port Lympne dried out, though a much smaller harbour remained in use at Hythe for another thousand years. By 1066 Romney had become an important port, though silting had already forced it to move three miles nearer the sea, and New Romney had already long eclipsed Old Romney.

Meanwhile the political importance of the narrow seas ports had become very great. They controlled trade, had fleets, and were rich. Although in name England was one kingdom both before and after 1066, the king had much trouble imposing unified rule on it. Both Anglo-Saxon and Norman monarchs took good care to earn the favour of these strategic towns, granting them rights and privileges beyond the ordinary. A Charter of Edward I in 1278 consolidated these already ancient statutes and established the Confederation of the Cinque Ports, which were Hastings, Romney, Hythe, Dover, and Sandwich, later joined by Rye and Winchelsea. This was the peak of Romney's importance. Its seamen and citizens, with their fellows in the Confederation, had great power, though some held them to be little but licensed pirates acting in the King's name though for their own benefit. But it was a short rule. Romney harbour was already under attack from the natural forces which had destroyed Lympne and were closing Hythe. During the Great Storm of 1287, the Rother changed its course again, and overnight began to flow into the sea at Rye. Without its water, Romney harbour was doomed, although it was another century before it became impractical for shipping, and much longer before it disappeared entirely. Indeed, the one-inch Ordnance Survey map in the 1880s still showed a small bay between the heads of Greatstone and Littlestone, a last remnant soon to vanish.

By the 15th century central government had begun to establish its power, and as the King came to have a navy of his own he needed the ships of the Cinque Ports less. Slowly, therefore, their jealously guarded rights and privileges dwindled into something purely ceremonial. New Romney, which had been the central meeting point and first among equals, turned its back on the sea and declined into a quiet farming town. Its church of St Nicholas, once on the harbour edge, is now over a mile from salt water. Similarly, the older part of Hythe, once situated on the first slopes of the hill above tidewater, is now half a mile from the front.

The most persistent Romney tradition between the decline of the Cinque Ports and modern times is smuggling, and of course conditions were ideal for it. The French coast was close, there were long stretches of wide and easy open beach to land on, and a flat windswept country behind on which the excisemen could be seen at a great distance. But for exactly the same reasons, it was perhaps the most obvious and easy landfall for an invading army. This threat was countered by Dover and Walmer Castles, while both Rye and Winchelsea were walled towns and equal strongpoints. The threat came closer in Napoleonic times, and more was done to meet it. The line of Martello Towers, small cannon-mounted forts, was hastily built between the cliffs at Folkestone and Dymchurch, and the Royal Military Canal, running along the inland edge of the whole Marsh from Hythe through Appledore to Winchelsea, was cut. This was designed as a line to be defended by infantry; but, since it had links with the sea at each end and since much of the Marsh, particularly further inland, was below sea level, its other purpose was to enable the land to be rapidly flooded in the event of an invasion.

None of these changes made much difference to the look of the land, except for the scattering of fine stone houses and churches built during periods of wealth. The remaining areas of marsh had been enclosed and drained between Roman times and the fifteenth century, the work continuing during the Dark Ages; but apart from these things there was no visible change until modern times began with the arrival of the railways. The South Eastern reached Folkestone from London in 1843, and Dover the following year. The first railway on the Marsh was the Ashford—Hastings line, opened shortly afterwards, which served Rye, Winchelsea, and (rather remotely) Appledore, skirting its inland edge. Into the heart of the Marsh there was nothing until the branch from Appledore was opened much later, reaching Lydd, Dungeness, and New Romney in 1883. Although it had been intended to carry this on through Dymchurch to Hythe, the work was never done. But all the same, the Marsh coastline was now accessible, and residential development began to create that ribbon of seaside houses, bungalows and shacks which line the coast at intervals between Hythe and Dungeness.

1
Principals and Prehistory

In March 1837 a young Englishman named Henry Howey, who had settled in New South Wales and who ran sheep on a property near Goulburn, about 140 miles south of Sydney, travelled overland to the newly-founded city of Melbourne, a journey which was still at that time quite adventurous. One of his reasons for going was to attend an auction at which land in what was intended to be the new city's centre was to be sold. He was successful in obtaining a number of plots, most of which he soon resold at a good profit, but he could not find a buyer for three of them, for which he had paid £128. They lay next to each other on low ground near the west bank of the Yarra River, and legend has it that the problem was that they were covered by a lot of trees too small to have any value and thus a nuisance which would have to be cleared; anyhow, he was left with them on his hands when he returned home. In 1838 he decided to move to Melbourne for good, taking his wife and six children; on 21 June, in poor weather, they all sailed from Sydney in the schooner *Sarah*. Neither the ship itself, nor any soul on board, was ever seen again. Howey had left no valid will, so that his estate, including the Melbourne land, in due course passed to his bachelor sea-captain brother in England, John Werge Howey.

John Howey held on to the land; no doubt he had a good idea of what it might be worth, since his ship sailed often enough to Australia. Over the years it was greatly developed, together with its surroundings, and eventually became a prime section of the central business district, bounded by Collins Street, Swanston Street, and Elizabeth Street, and within a short distance of the main railway station at Flinders Street. It was of great value; indeed it has been claimed that it became the most valuable privately owned section of land in any city of the British Empire. On John Howey's death, still a bachelor, in 1871, when it was already worth over a million pounds, it passed to his nephew, John Edwards Werge Howey, an officer in the Indian Army.

In due course J.E.W. Howey resigned his commission and returned to England, married, and settled at Melford Grange, near Woodbridge, Suffolk. There, on 17 November 1886, his eldest son, John Edwards Presgrave Howey, was born. Three daughters followed, and another son, Richard, in 1896.

Woodbridge is a delightful small town still, and life at Melford Grange, in comfortable circumstances, must have been very pleasant. Things mechanical interested Howey senior; there was a succession of cars from the mid-1890s, and a steam launch for family outings on the River Deben. The East Suffolk line of the Great Eastern Railway passed quite close to the house, and among the household possessions there was certainly a rather fine Gauge 1 tinplate model railway. All these things delighted the sons as much as their father. In spite of the difference in age, John and Richard were better friends than brothers sometimes are, and the older had a small seat added to his bicycle so that they could go out riding together.

J.E.P. Howey was in due course sent off to preparatory school and then Eton. It is perhaps understandable that he did adequately but not remarkably in the completely non-technical type of education then on offer in almost all public schools, showing enthusiasm only at games. At Eton he made friends with the grandson of the great railway-building Duke of Sutherland, who had paid nearly all the cost of building the Inverness to Wick and Thurso line out of his own pocket; both boys shared an interest in railways. On leaving Eton Howey was for a while a premium apprentice at Vickers, but this experiment, then quite remarkable in an ex-Etonian, was not a success. Instead he set about enjoying life in a way perhaps easier in those last few years before 1914 than at any time since, spending much of the time in Sutherland, where he became an excellent shot. 1911 was his *annus mirabilis*. He made his first journey to Australia; he commissioned to be built an impressive 60hp Napier car; and from the famous Northampton firm of Bassett-Lowke he took delivery of a $9\frac{1}{2}$in gauge model of a Great Northern Railway Ivatt Atlantic, one-sixth scale size. As he said later, he wanted something he could ride in. Finally, he married Gladys Hewitt, and moved into a house close to Melford Grange. His parents had the previous year moved away from the bracing gales of the East Coast to Surrey, but Howey still loved Woodbridge.

However, the most formative event of the year occurred on 1 May. On that day the Rhyl Miniature Railway was opened, and as a valued customer of Bassett-Lowke Howey was invited to

Sir Arthur Heywood's line at Duffield Bank, apart from demonstrating its builder's ideas, was probably the finest garden railway there has ever been. His 0-6-0T *Ella* poses on the 25ft radius curve on the 1 in 12 grade, some time in the 1890s.

attend. He spent much of the day driving the railway's first locomotive, one of the 15in gauge Bassett-Lowke Little Giant Atlantics, half as big again as his own engine, and in his own words he 'caught the fifteen-inch-gauge bug.' There was something much more impressive about it. At Woodbridge he could steam up and down one side of the garden, sitting on a trolley behind his 9½in gauge engine, pulling or pushing perhaps half a dozen children. At Rhyl there was a well-engineered circular track on which a locomotive could be properly opened up and reach a good speed. The driver could sit inside the cab (even if he had to look forward along the top of the boiler), and 40 or 50 adults would be riding in the train. Driving a sizeable steam locomotive for the first time is a dangerous experience; once a man has opened the regulator and felt the iron horse stir into life beneath his hand, he is a changed soul. Something like this happened that day to Howey; a yeast was set fermenting in his brain which ultimately set the course of his career.

At this point it is perhaps useful to give a short account of some of the other people then active in the miniature railway business, with most of whom Howey had dealings then or later. The Grand Old Man of the 15in gauge railway was certainly Sir Arthur Heywood (1849–1916), one

of the first graduates of the School of Engineering at Cambridge University, who had settled on that gauge as the narrowest which could guarantee the stability of a passenger coach regardless of how the occupants moved about, and who devoted most of his life to an effort to persuade people that railways of this size were the ideal means of moving freight, and occasionally passengers, to and from a main line in cases where there was not enough traffic to justify a full-sized branch. He had only a limited success in this endeavour, but he owned a remarkably fine private workshop, with a skilled staff, and to demonstrate his ideas built in the grounds of his house at Duffield, near Derby, perhaps the finest garden railway the world has ever seen. It was 15in gauge, of course, and had tunnels, viaducts, horseshoe curves and alpine gradients, stations and signalboxes and sheds; it had three highly individual and effective steam locomotives, all kinds of wagons and a stock of coaches which included a dining car and a sleeping car. He also had enough children for them to be able to staff the whole operation and run trains at fever pitch. Very occasionally he opened his line to the public, and word of its wonders spread far and wide. However effective a railway of this kind might be as an economical means of shifting coal or gravel, though, the most evident thing about it was that it was tremendous fun.

The only railway which Heywood ever built to put his ideas into practice was a three-mile line at Eaton Hall, near Chester, in 1896. Its main function was to carry coal and other goods between Balderton station, the Hall, and other parts of the Duke of Westminster's Eaton Estate. It had a few coaches and sometimes ran trains for parties or charities; on one occasion Winston Churchill, a guest at the Hall and not a very good shot, crept away from the shooting party where he had been missing too many birds for comfort and had a much pleasanter afternoon riding up and down on the engine. So even at Eaton things were not wholly serious. Heywood should not have been surprised, even if he was a little disappointed, that the main result of his efforts was that 15in gauge miniature railways, from the 1890s on, became great popular attractions in parks and pleasure gardens in many parts of the world. But the reason for his disappointment would have been, not any feeling that mere entertainment was an unworthy use of his ideas, but simply the low standard of engineering and design of most of these lines. Heywood's idea had been to build locomotives and stock that were strong and simple, designed for economical service, and in no way to make a model of any full-size prototype. Operators of pleasure railways, on the other hand, tended to start with the assumption that the little train had to resemble

Sir Arthur Heywood beside his first 15in gauge locomotive, at Duffield Bank in the mid-1870s.

the big one if it was to draw the public, even if the resemblance was so crude that it was really more of a caricature.

Leading the business of building locomotives for pleasure lines in the early years of the century were the Cagney brothers in New York, who mass-produced a large number of solid and serviceable, but very rough-looking and generally quite tiny engines obviously intended to look like traditional American 4–4–0s. Most of these were to 15in gauge, and they were exported all over the world.

Two of them came to England, and in 1903 arrived at Blakesley Hall, near Northampton, where C. W. Bartholomew, the squire, laid down a line from the Hall to Blakesley station on the Stratford-on-Avon & Midland Junction Railway, of which small company he was a director. There was a telephone by which guests arriving on the SMJ could summon a train to take them to the Hall, which might turn out to be driven by the butler. But mainly this was a fun railway, and as such it struck the imagination of W. J Bassett-Lowke, who visited Blakesley. Bassett-Lowke's family had an engineering and boilermaking works in Northampton, but his own interest was in making and selling models, and he was developing this activity into a substantial little business. The main part of his effort was in

The little 4–4–0s built by the Cagney brothers of New York were crude and tiny, but commercially very successful. One of the Blakesley Hall engines, on a visit to New Romney in 1969, alongside *Doctor Syn*. (*G. A. Barlow*)

making and marketing toy trains, in gauges up to $2\frac{1}{2}$in, but Bassett-Lowke was also interested in the increasingly popular model engineering hobby, and wanted to deal in much larger models. The Cagneys had made a commercial success of them, and so could he.

An important part was being played in the development of the model engineering hobby by its main mouthpiece, the magazine *Model Engineer*, happily still with us, which had been founded in 1898 by Percival Marshall. One of its main contributors was Henry Greenly, a young man (born in 1876) who had left a job with good career prospects working for the Metropolitan Railway, and who to the dismay of his parents was devoting himself to the design of models of all kinds, but chiefly steam locomotives. Bassett-Lowke commissioned Greenly in 1901 to design some British-type tinplate toy locomotives for him which, even if at first they would generally have to be manufactured in Germany, would resemble the originals better than the travesties which Bing and Märklin had begun to sell in Britain. Business prospered, and Bassett-Lowke indoor model railways had by 1910, thanks in part to Greenly's sure touch which practically amounted to genius, developed into probably the best commercially available in the world. Greenly shared Bassett-Lowke's wish to expand his product range upwards in size, and he designed bigger and bigger models for him. Most of Greenly's writing, both for the *Model Engineer* and his own

magazine *Models, Railways, and Locomotives* which he started in 1909, dealt with railways of between $1\frac{1}{4}$in and 5in gauge, though larger sizes were described whenever the opportunity arose.

The problem was one of marketing. The potential sale for indoor or table-top model railways was very considerable, but it reduced as the models got bigger. Lines to run them on took up much more room, and of course expense mounted; 5in (or $4\frac{3}{4}$in) gauge, at a scale of one inch to the foot, was about as large as the most dedicated model engineer wanted to go. One-eighth scale ($7\frac{1}{4}$ or $7\frac{1}{2}$in gauge), and one-sixth ($9\frac{1}{2}$ or $10\frac{1}{4}$in gauge) were relatively enormous, and very few customers could be found for locomotives in these sizes, though as we have seen J. E. P. Howey was one of them. Yet both these sizes were still really too small for the commercial operator; 15in gauge, or roughly quarter scale, provided the smallest machines which could earn a worthwhile revenue. It followed that, although Bassett-Lowke was willing to build in any size to special order, to do any quarter-scale work would mean getting into the whole field of designing, building, and operating 15in gauge railways.

For this reason, Bassett-Lowke and a number of collaborators in 1904 started a company, Miniature Railways of Great Britain Ltd. Greenly designed for the new company its first 15in gauge locomotive, a 4–4–2 named *Little Giant*, somewhat reminiscent of a North Eastern Railway Atlantic. It was quite a small engine, weighing complete and in working order only about $1\frac{3}{4}$ tons; its dimensions were those of a scale model, and like most main-line engines of its day it had a narrow firebox lying between the frames.

The new company did not prosper, and eventually failed in 1912. Its first line was a circular affair on the beach at Blackpool, which lasted only from 1905 to 1907, when its equipment was moved to Halifax Zoo in Yorkshire. In 1908 another line was built in a park at Sutton Coldfield, and another identical engine, named *Mighty Atom*, built for it. But by this time Greenly had had enough experience with *Little Giant* to realise that it lacked power. It could pull 30 or 40 people on the level at 20mph, but this was not enough for commercial service, particularly as few lines were as level as all that. Subsequent engines of the Little Giant type had bigger boilers, and it was one of these which opened the Rhyl Miniature Railway in 1911. But Greenly was still dissatisfied; he felt that something even better was needed, and later that same year he designed another 15in gauge Atlantic approximately 25 per cent bigger and more powerful. As it happened, only three of these *Sans Pareil* class locomotives were built, but they were of crucial importance in the development of Greenly's thinking because for the first time he applied the principle of building larger than scale. With considerable skill he designed the engine so that it still looked like a scale model, but it was no such thing; its major dimensions were much too big to be 'correct'. Like the full-size locomotive engineer, in fact, and against the model engineering ethic, Greenly had begun to design for power and capacity rather than looks. Perhaps his work in connection with the $9\frac{1}{2}$in gauge Ivatt Atlantic which Bassett-Lowke was building for Howey reminded him of the advantage, for steam-producing capacity, of the wide-firebox boiler

overlapping the frames, which the Great Northern was at that time almost the only British railway to use; certainly the *Sans Pareil* class had a wide firebox, and somewhat resembled the Ivatt design.

Howey did not remain long in the house at Woodbridge; during 1912 he began to look for a bigger property, where he could build himself a much longer railway on which he could repeat the Rhyl experience. That autumn he leased and moved into Staughton Manor, in Huntingdonshire. At once he commissioned Greenly to build the new line, which was to be $\frac{3}{4}$-mile from end to end. The site allowed for a later extension to form a circle with about $1\frac{1}{2}$ miles of track, though this was never built. One remarkable feature was a large cantilever bridge, reminiscent of the Forth Bridge, with a 20ft span. Perhaps out of a lingering sense of economy, but more probably because for all his admiration of the Rhyl line Howey instinctively felt that the Little Giants were no good (in later years he always described them as 'dreadful little things'), he stuck to the $9\frac{1}{2}$in gauge and kept his model Ivatt Atlantic. Work on the Staughton Manor line continued through that winter, and it was completed during the spring; during summer 1912 it was properly photographed and shown off to many visitors, including parties of local children. But economy was about to be thrown out of the window, for Howey was suddenly upstaged by a complete stranger.

The offender was Sir Robert Walker, a friend of Heywood's who lived at Sand Hutton Hall, some eight miles east of York. During 1911 he began to build in his grounds a 15in gauge line, quite steeply graded, $\frac{2}{3}$-mile long. He intended it

J. E. P. Howey and his $9\frac{1}{2}$in gauge Greenly/Bassett-Lowke Atlantic, at Staughton Manor in 1912, plus the first of his railway dogs.

Howey on his Gigantic class 4–6–2, when running on the Eaton Railway in 1914, beside the Heywood 0–4–0T *Katie*. The man in the bowler hat is Fred Green, Bassett-Lowke's foreman.

to be the first stage of a considerable system of about eight miles, linking Sand Hutton, Bossall, and several other villages, plus a brickworks, with the North Eastern Railway at Warthill on the York–Hull line, but to build this involved long legal delays. (The line was ultimately completed after the war, but on the 18in gauge, using second-hand War Department stock, and so hardly in fact as a miniature railway). Walker was another client of Bassett-Lowke, and on learning of Greenly's design for the *Sans Pareil* Atlantic promptly ordered the first one; possibly with guile, he named it *Synolda* after his wife. When delivered in 1912, it proved to be everything Greenly had intended, and a radical improvement on *Little Giant*. Cecil J. Allen described its performance in *The Railway Magazine* in glowing terms, and although the model engineering papers wrote up the Staughton Manor line at the same time, they hardly had the same class. There was no denying it; Howey had been outmatched.

This would never do. Perhaps the Atlantic type was the prime British express train locomotive of the day, but something bigger and better was looming on the horizon, the Pacific. Indeed, the Great Western Railway had already built one. Howey would have the second. Consultations with Greenly and Bassett-Lowke followed, and a design was prepared for a 'stretched' version of *Sans Pareil*, with a third pair of driving wheels and bigger boiler and cylinders. This went into

the Bassett-Lowke catalogue as the Gigantic class. All this took time, during which Howey must have fretted; but by the end of 1913 the Staughton Manor Railway was relaid to 15in gauge and the Forth Bridge strengthened to take what was at that time certainly the biggest model locomotive ever built, weighing over three tons. The machine itself was delivered just before the end of the year, the Ivatt going back to Bassett-Lowke in part exchange.

Only one Gigantic 4–6–2 was ever made, although there was some confusion about this. It was properly named *John Anthony* after Howey's son (who had been born in 1912), but Bassett-Lowke had it photographed for his catalogue and retouched the print so that the nameplates read *Gigantic*. Twenty-five percent bigger again than *Synolda*, it was claimed to be capable of hauling 150 people at 30mph. Howey was leading the field once more. But the Staughton Manor line was too short for him to be able to show his engine's paces properly, and after some months he arranged for it to have a period of trial running on the Eaton Railway. This was much the longest and best-maintained 15in gauge line in Britain, three miles in length and with track as smooth as a billiard table. Here during July Howey worked *John Anthony* with a light train up to a maximum of 34.6mph, certainly the equivalent of over 100mph for any full-sized locomotive, and hauled some quite impressive loads at lower speeds. Cecil J. Allen was invited along, and later did his duty in *The Railway Magazine*. Honour in the matter of Sir Robert Walker was thus satisfied. At the end of the month, leaving his engine at Eaton, Howey travelled up to Scotland for the shooting, but shooting of a far more serious kind began that August. He was soon summoned south again for the mobilisation of the Bedfordshire Yeomanry, a territorial regiment in which he held a commission.

Not many of the young men in their twenties who answered the call to arms in August 1914 were still alive when the first world war ended in November 1918. Howey was one of the lucky ones. Given his interests, it is not surprising that he was one of the first volunteers for transfer to the Royal Flying Corps. He was not however to achieve his intention of qualifying as a pilot. He flew, but as an observer with 6 Squadron, RFC, based at Abeele, just inside Belgium. Fortunately he observed the pilot and how he flew the machine as well as movements behind enemy lines. On 11 November 1915 he was flying in an FE2 biplane, a twin-cockpit two-seater in which the observer sat ahead of the pilot. Over Rolleghem they were attacked by a German fighter, but managed to damage it so that it had to land. Then Howey noticed the plane was behaving strangely, and looked round to find to his horror that the pilot, Second Lt C. H. Kelway-Bamber, had been hit and was dead. Knowing that he was a dead man himself unless he managed to bring the plane down safely, he scrambled back over the pilot's body and succeeded in landing, or more accurately crashing gently, suffering nothing worse than being thrown clear and knocked out. But he had, understandably, come down behind the German lines. When he recovered consciousness he found himself staring down a German rifle.

He had a bad time as a prisoner of war, being taken round between various camps and displayed in a humiliating way. Doubtless the Germans had done their homework on finding out who he was, and had decided that it would be a good thing for national morale to see a captive English millionaire being spat on. Fortunately his luck turned eventually. He was declared medically unfit for military service in mid-1917, and released on parole to Switzerland. There after a little while he was joined by his wife Gladys, who instantly sent packing the wife of the prison camp doctor who had certified him unfit, who was staying in the same hotel. And there he had to remain until the war ended.

Greenly had a less eventful war, most of which was spent at the Royal Aircraft Factory at Farnborough, designing among other things equipment to enable machine guns to be mounted and used effectively from the air. Only Bassett-Lowke was able to continue with his railway interests, but in 1915 he pulled off his greatest coup.

The seven-mile 3ft gauge Ravenglass & Eskdale Railway in the Lake District had closed in 1913 and was lying derelict. Bassett-Lowke conceived the idea of taking it over and converting it to 15in gauge. He was now connected with a new company, Narrow Gauge Railways Ltd, and he had several Little Giant engines, one Sans Pareil, and a number of coaches left on his hands. A lease of the R&ER was arranged, and by the end of the year 15in gauge trains were running from Ravenglass to Irton Road. Things looked promising, except for the fact that for a (relatively) long and steeply-graded railway the shortcomings of the Bassett-Lowke engines were all too obvious; indeed, no attempt to use any of the Little Giants was made at all. With the reopening of practically the whole of the old line due the following spring, there was a desperate shortage of serviceable equipment.

Proctor Mitchell, the Manager of the R&ER, persuaded Howey, then captive in Germany, to sell *John Anthony*, and at the same time purchased another engine which had seen service on the Eaton Railway. Howey's monster was renamed *Colossus*. Sir Arthur Heywood died in early 1916, and NGR managed to obtain almost all the locomotives and rolling stock from Duffield Bank. Bassett-Lowke's project also created a great deal of interest, and undoubtedly sparked off the idea of doing the same thing on a much grander scale. The Eskdale line, after all, was a byway, however enchanting.

The earliest conception of the idea of building a miniature main line railway seems to have been about 1918 or 1919, in Bassett-Lowke's famous shop at 112 Holborn, in London. It was visited one day by the Grand Duke Dmitri Pavlovitch of Russia, cousin of Czar Nicholas II and one of the assassins of Rasputin, and Count Louis Zborowski. Both men were in their twenties, and got into a discussion of the Eskdale project with R. H. Fuller, then a young assistant with the firm. The converation impressed Fuller so vividly that he recalled it 60 years later. The two visitors were fired by the vision of such a line with double track, signalling, fast trains, and all the trimmings. It was of course exactly the kind of mad romantic idea to have appealed to the Slav imagination, and not a British sort of concept at all. But Russia was taking another path and had no opportunity for frivolities of that sort again. Meanwhile, by fits and starts the Ravenglass & Eskdale came

Howey driving his Leyland Eight on the public road near Brooklands, June 1923. (*National Motor Museum*)

back to life. This, though, is not the place to expand on its history, which has been admirably told elsewhere. But one matter does concern us.

Experience soon showed that even *Sans Pareil* and *Colossus* were not up to the work. Although beefed-up by 25 percent, the scale model locomotives simply had not enough power, and lacked mechanical robustness. Passengers on a summer jaunt might not mind having to get out and push up the steeper hills, but this was no way to run a railway with a year-round commercial passenger and freight service. The Heywood engines were much better, but even they suffered from Sir Arthur's predilection for marine-type boilers, which were simpler in construction than the classic locomotive boiler but lacked the latter's ability to produce large amounts of steam when forced. Seeing which way the wind was blowing, and in any case being more interested in his model manufacturing business, Bassett-Lowke quietly faded from the 15in scene. But Greenly was made of sterner stuff. He became quite heavily involved with the R&ER after 1918 and showed his mettle as a general engineering all-rounder by designing for its new quarrying activities a granite-crushing

plant and some heavy-duty wagons and tranship facilities. The line had in 1919 taken delivery of another Pacific, a machine closely resembling *Colossus*, named *Sir Aubrey Brocklebank*, but this was also inadequate; so in 1922 Greenly designed something radically better.

This locomotive, the 2–8–2 *River Esk*, was delivered in 1923. It was practically twice the weight and power of *Colossus*, scaling almost seven tons complete and in working order. It was again a freelance design, although it looked as if it could have been a model of a heavy-duty main-line British 2–8–2 of the period, if such a thing had existed. But it was built to one-third scale, not the one-quarter which corresponded with the 15in gauge. Much of the extra weight did not go to producing extra power but into extra mechanical strength; heavy frames, generous bearings and journals, altogether an exceptionally tough and solid machine, following Heywood's teaching in this direction. Bassett-Lowke had been ruled out of court as a possible builder; instead, the firm of Davey, Paxman of Colchester was chosen. It was rather an odd choice in some ways; they were certainly in a substantial class as engineers, but had never previously built a locomotive. They had, however, built traction engines. Their main trade was in marine machinery and they were already beginning to emphasise diesel power; in

Louis Zborowski at the wheel of a 135hp Mercedes, at Brooklands in 1923. (*National Motor Museum*)

fact the truth of the matter was that the Chairman of the R&ER, Sir Aubrey Brocklebank, also happened to be the Chairman of the Cunard Steamship Company, and Paxmans were prepared to indulge an important customer. *River Esk* had some bad times at first, as Greenly made the mistake of allowing Paxmans to fit Lentz poppet valves and gear, a design in which they had an interest, in return for a reduction on the price. Once these had been replaced by ordinary piston valves with Walschaerts gear the locomotive was a complete success, and is still running.

On returning to circulation after the war, Howey for a while abandoned his railway interests. At his wife's urging, he took a house in Belgravia (31 Pont Street) and became something of a man-about-London, developing a keen interest in the theatre and in social life with theatre people. He bought a motor torpedo boat, and took to charging round Southampton Water with his friends at 40 knots. He had another house at Sunningdale, with an enormous model railway in the garage which his son and his friends were not allowed to touch. But a much more serious new interest was in motor racing, centred on the

famous Brooklands track at Weybridge.

His career as a Brooklands driver was relatively short; he did not have his own racing car until 1923, when he took delivery of a 7-litre Leyland rebuilt for him by Parry Thomas. On the whole he did well enough on the track for honour to be satisfied, but not well enough to shine; perhaps his instinct for mechanical things held him back short of the slightly suicidal zone in which the real glories are won. He was also, at 37, a little old for the game, particularly as a newcomer to it. His brother Richard, at 27, took up the sport at the same time, and did perhaps a little better in competition.

The most important result of Howey's involvement with fast cars was that in 1921 he met Count Louis Zborowski, who had appeared at Brooklands that season and created a sensation by lapping at 108mph in his first race with his amazing 23-litre Mercedes-Maybach, *Chitty-Chitty-Bang-Bang*, named after the noise it made when starting up. This was the first of four similarly-named, vicious, aeroplane-engined and legendary monsters which only Zborowski could really control; all were quite unlike the milksop vehicle seen in the cinema 50 years later. Zborowski was a remarkable man, eight years younger than Howey, and an irrepressible ball of fire with a keen sense of fun which sometimes

J. A. Holder, of Broome, Worcestershire, purchased Howey's old Atlantic and altered it to 10¼in gauge. Here his son Terry, later Manager of the RH&DR, brings in the hay crop with an earlier Atlantic, about 1913. (*J. A. Holder*)

showed itself in slightly malicious set-piece practical jokes at the expense of people who seemed to take life too seriously. One such person, staying with a group at Zborowski's place for the weekend, was sent out to the swimming pool on some errand while the rest of the guests watched from indoors. As he stood by the water, Zborowski to everyone's astonishment produced a long-handled dynamo exploder and proceeded to detonate a home-made depth charge which had been laid in the pool some time earlier. Fortunately it was only the water, and not the lumps of shattered concrete, that rose in a tall column before descending on the wretched victim.

Zborowski's name and title were ·Polish, though until 1919 this had meant Russian; but his mother was American, and since his father had been killed motor-racing many years earlier, he had had an Anglo-American upbringing. Like Howey, he had gone to Eton, and was deeply interested in things mechanical. He had a large well-staffed workshop of his own, where he built and maintained his fleet of 30 or so exceptional

cars, and he had been one of the founders of the Aston Martin Motor Company. Perhaps more to the point, he was rich on a scale that made Howey look impoverished. Howey owned a good slice of the middle of Melbourne, but Zborowski's mother was an Astor, and the Astors owned a good deal of the middle of New York.

The two men became close friends, and at some point, finding that Howey was also interested in 15in gauge railways, Zborowski told him of his vision of a main line in miniature. In June 1924 they visited the Ravenglass & Eskdale Railway. This was something after the hearts of both, and their first thought was to see whether they could buy the line, then improve and extend it. But here they ran into a stone wall just as solid as the mountain barrier at the head of the Esk Valley. The legal and financial affairs of the railway were in a great muddle, Bassett-Lowke having leased the old abandoned formation from a shareholder of the old company who had no proper authority to grant it, while its mechanical state was little better. A strong man had already moved in to sort matters out, and was determined to do so in his own way; and Sir Aubrey Brocklebank, if not in quite the same category of the extremely rich, was adequately breeched for the purpose. There was a personal awkwardness as well. Brocklebank

Greenly's *River Esk* leaving Ravenglass in the late 1920s. By this time the engine had already been rebuilt once, exchanging its original Lentz valve gear and cylinders for piston valves and Walschaerts gear; from 1927 to 1930, as here, it also ran coupled to an 0–8–0 steam tender. (*W. H. Whitworth*)

The only one of his engines that Zborowski lived to see finished was sold after his death to the Fairbourne Railway and named *Count Louis*. In 1980 the 4–4–2 finally visited the RH&DR and is seen here passing *Hurricane* at Botolph's Bridge. (*J. B. Snell*)

criticised Howey to his face for having asked the high price of £800 when selling *John Anthony* to the R&ER, twice what it had cost; and although he did so good-humouredly, he must have felt quite strongly to have raised the subject at all. Howey was indignant, protesting that he had asked only £400, and eventually it transpired that Proctor Mitchell, who had by that time disappeared from the scene, had kept the difference for himself.

However, there was another item on the agenda. Zborowski was building a 15in gauge line in the considerable grounds of his estate at Bridge, near Canterbury, and had during 1924 acquired the third and last Sans Pareil Atlantic, which had been lying unfinished in the Bassett-Lowke works since before the war. He was determined to have another engine, to be the best and biggest miniature locomotive ever built, and to include all the improvements which Eskdale experience had suggested. Henry Greenly was the obvious man to consult. During discussions between Zborowski, Howey, and Greenly earlier in 1924, an outline specification had been hammered out for a 15in gauge Pacific, built approximately to one-third scale, following the general principles of *River Esk* in regard to size, power, and robustness, though with some advance on all three points. Which of the three men decided on the quite considerable further increase in the sizes of bearings, bushes, journals and axleboxes is not recorded, but this was a significant step and was probably Zborowski's contribution. Howey was not interested in such details, and Greenly probably felt he had got them right on *River Esk*; but Zborowski with his workshop experience and American background is the most likely one of the three to have wanted it. The fact remains that the Eskdale visit confirmed the whole matter, and in July 1924 Zborowski, never a man to do things by halves, placed an order with Paxmans for not one but two locomotives to this specification. It seems likely that one was intended for Howey, but Paxman's records show clearly that Zborowski ordered both, and to this day each carries the identification LZ1 or LZ2 stamped on its rods and valve gear.

However, one or other of the two insisted that the locomotives should not be completely freelance in design, as Greenly usually preferred, but should resemble as closely as possible the Gresley Pacifics of the London & North Eastern Railway, the first of which had appeared on the Great Northern Railway in 1922 and were certainly the most impressive, and arguably the best, British express locomotives of the day. But then, on 19 October 1924, Zborowski was killed while driving in the Italian Grand Prix at Monza, and everything was cast into doubt.

2
Finding the Site

Zborowski's death would probably have stopped Howey's return to the miniature railway world had it not been for two things. One was that Howey's father had died some months earlier, and so now he was his own master as far as finding large sums of money was concerned. The other was the encouragement of friends who shared his interest. Two among these were important. Kenelm Lee Guinness was a Brooklands star of the first order, who had broken the British land speed record by driving at 133mph in 1922. The other was J. A. Holder, member of a family of Midlands brewers, who had a very fine $10\frac{1}{4}$in gauge railway on his estate at Broome, in Worcestershire, and who had got to know Howey after acquiring his old Ivatt Atlantic. Holder set up the miniature railway in the grounds of the Wembley Empire Exhibition in 1925, and his teenage son Terence spent most of that summer as one of its drivers. Howey's mother was all in favour of encouraging his interest in railways, on the grounds that they were a great deal safer than fast cars; moreover there was also the fact that Davey, Paxman were pressing on with their contract and the locomotives would soon be available anyhow. Finally, a railway would be a memorial to Zborowski. Howey later said that this was his main motive. So early in 1925 Greenly was commissioned to find a place to build it. There was only one condition; it would have to be the best in the world. This meant that it would not only have to be longer than the Eskdale, seven miles at least, but also straight and level enough to allow its trains to go really fast.

To build any railway of this length it would be essential to have power of compulsory purchase of

Ex Works: Howey stands alongside *Green Goddess*, still with blank nameplates, newly completed at Davey, Paxman's.

land, and so obtaining Parliamentary authority under the Light Railway Order procedure. This would never be forthcoming unless the line was going to be of some public benefit, so there had to be some genuine unsatisfied public demand for rail transport on the chosen site. There were not many places in Britain where this situation obtained in 1925; rails reached almost everywhere and hardly any branch had closed. The list would be reduced even further if it were confined to flat country. However, Greenly discovered two places with possibilities.

One was at Brean Sands, in Somerset, between Burnham-on-Sea and Weston-super-Mare. This would allow a main line of just over seven miles, flat and straight enough, but requiring a substantial bridge over the River Axe. A map in Greenly's surviving papers shows its course as commencing on the inland side of Burnham, some little way from the terminus of the Somerset & Dorset Railway branch which served the town. It then connected with the main Bristol and Exeter line of the Great Western Railway at Brent Knoll station before following its own route, parallel but at some distance from the GWR, to a separate station on the outskirts of Weston. A branch line to the Brean Down peninsula was pencilled in. The area was beginning to develop as a place for summer holidays, but all the same there was no real case for saying that the railway would be of

much public benefit, nor did the GWR take kindly to the idea of any competition. Greenly had correspondence with Felix Pole, the General Manager, about the project, but got no encouragement.

The second possibility was to follow the Eskdale precedent and take over an existing railway. In those days, of course, abandoned lines were very rare, and it was unlikely that any large company would be willing to sell even the most moribund of its tentacles; but there were some small companies which might. One prospect was the Hundred of Manhood & Selsey Tramway, which ran the $7\frac{3}{4}$ miles of standard gauge light railway from Chichester to Selsey, in Sussex. This would have filled the bill admirably, and ought to have been for sale as it was visibly failing (although in the event it managed to struggle on for another 10 years). But the difficulty was just that the line *was* still running, more or less, and the local people were in no mood to exchange a full-sized railway which they knew for something else. The redoubtable Colonel Stephens, Manager, Receiver, and Engineer of the Selsey line as well as a dozen or so similar railways in England and Wales, was not an easy man to convince either. So that idea came to nothing.

Meanwhile Davey, Paxman had completed the two locomotives. Howey and Greenly arranged to take the first one, which had been named *Green Goddess*, up to Ravenglass for trials on the Eskdale line which took place during June and July 1925. They were a considerable success, with *Green Goddess* achieving a maximum of 35mph

Green Goddess on test on the Ravenglass & Eskdale in 1925, posed in scenery highly unlike that in which she later settled. (*J. T. Holder*)

and hauling a train with 160 passengers up the difficult gradients; she considerably out-performed *River Esk*, though it is fair to say that at the time *River Esk* was still suffering from its defective Lentz valves. Howey invited a number of friends along for a celebratory special run, though any idea of exhibiting *Green Goddess* alongside his 1913 Pacific *Colossus*, had to be dropped as the older machine had just been badly bent in a head-on collision with a stone train hauled by one of Heywood's engines. In fact, operating practices on the R&ER left something to be desired, and *Green Goddess* only narrowly avoided a similar fate, which might have shaken Howey's mother's preference for trains over motor cars.

Then, in August 1925, Greenly went to see Sir Herbert Walker, General Manager of the Southern Railway, at Waterloo. Alone among the big four companies, the Southern was at that time still expansion-minded. The others were already becoming defensive and cautious, as road competition began to bite, but the SR was experiencing great increases in traffic and profitability as the result of electrification. Sir Herbert had just reviewed the whole system to determine where there was potential for new

lines. One place which came under study was Romney Marsh, where the South Eastern had obtained powers in 1884 to build from New Romney to Hythe, and where a standard-gauge light railway or electric tramway had been proposed in 1906 without result. There was still a feeling in favour of a railway, particularly in Dymchurch, but all the indications were that a full-sized line would never pay. It seemed to Sir Herbert that this might be just the place for Howey's project.

Things happened fast in those days, at least if fund raising was not a problem. Greenly immediately went down to New Romney to have a look, and reported favourably on Walker's proposal to Howey. The route was eight miles long, level, and without any important obstacles. On 8 September Howey visited New Romney for the first time, and agreed then and there to proceed. The local newspapers had the story within days, and published the fact that it was intended to build to the 15in gauge and to use the two Howey/Zborowski engines, of which pictures appeared. During October the second machine was purchased from Zborowski's executors, and on the first of that month Greenly moved down to New Romney where he took rooms at the Station Hotel and rented the billiard room to use as a drawing office. He set to work to survey the line. By 11 November this task was completed, plans and notices published and delivered to all landowners and local authorities affected, and on 14 November a formal application for a Light Railway Order was sent off to the Ministry of Transport.

Then began a period of horse-trading, settling points of disagreement so far as possible by negotiation. Interested parties were the Southern Railway, the various local councils, the affected landowners, and the bus company. Greenly's original intention had been to build a terminal station for the new railway on the north side of Littlestone Road, opposite the SR station, with a 15in gauge siding crossing the road into the SR yard for exchanging goods traffic. The Southern objected to this, and said they would prefer to see their own main platform track extended across the road as a siding into the narrow-gauge yard, which Greenly agreed to.

The various local councils were all generally in favour of the scheme, but made objection to certain details. The Kent County Council wanted an assurance that there would be facilities to handle ballast traffic from the pits near Hythe, and refused to accept the original proposal for a

Green Goddess at Ravenglass in July 1925. With it, left to right, are: Hugh Simpson of *The Locomotive Magazine*, Clive Gallop (Zborowski's motoring manager), Richard Howey, J. A. Holder, J. T. Holder, Henry Greenly and (in cab) J. E. P. Howey. *(J. T. Holder)*

level crossing with the main coast road at The Warren. They very rightly insisted on a bridge. Observing their success, Hythe Town Council demanded another bridge, to carry West Hythe road over the line at the Prince of Wales Inn. To this Howey did not at first agree, and finally this bridge was imposed by the Ministry. The worst problem however was with the New Romney Town Council, even though feeling in the borough was predominantly in favour of the line. The Mayor at that time was one Mr Luxmoor, KC, who presumably felt it his duty as a lawyer to give the railway a run for its money, and made a number of difficulties. One of them related to the level crossing at Littlestone Road, which would, he said, be a serious vexation with the gates closed frequently to allow long spasms of shunting. Greenly could make no headway in arguing his case with so senior a legal eagle, and finally had to agree to a unique limitation being inserted in the Light Railway Order that the crossing could only be used by goods trains, and not more than twice a day in each direction.

However, the railway won the next round. Howey was impatient with tedious legalities and wanted to get work started at once. *Green Goddess* had been brought down to New Romney

and was on public display in Binns' Garage, next to the station; now he wanted to see some track down, and a station building. After a prolonged siege, the farmer who rented from the SR the field on which New Romney station was to be built agreed at the beginning of December to give it up and the SR was expected to sell it at once. Hearing of this, on 5 December Mr Luxmoor delivered an edict that under no circumstances could any work be done until the Light Railway Order had been granted. Nonsense, said Howey, the land is mine, freehold, and at my own risk I can do what I like with it, and on 8 December the Ministry confirmed that this was so. Ground had already been broken, and before Christmas photographs had appeared of Greenly at work with a theodolite, Howey superintending, and newly-laid track in the background.

There were rather more problems with landowners. Greenly beavered away and saw them all one by one. All the 16 acres of land required were agricultural, and could be adversely affected in two ways. A field cut by a railway becomes two fields. If arable land, this might mean one or both becoming too small to plough economically; if pasture, the same factor could apply, but one field could also be made useless by being separated from water. All these matters could be settled by compensation on well-established principles, and sometimes ameliorated by generous provision of occupation crossings or bridges under or over the track. But such calculations were spoilt by the fact that building

19

development was beginning to push up land values. Grazing land on the Marsh was at that time worth perhaps £50 an acre, but land for building was changing hands at £700 an acre or more. Some owners understandably hated to lose the prospect of profits of this order because a railway would take their land instead, at a much lower price. Their fury was fanned to white heat on discovering what kind of a railway was planned, and who was proposing to build it. At the same time, the East Kent Road Car Company was most upset about having to face a new competitor. The local political cauldron began to bubble, and although numerous public meetings passed resolutions in favour, it was clear that the application for the Light Railway Order would be hotly opposed.

Meanwhile, the draft Order was being composed by Alan D. Erskine, of the Light Railways Department at the Board of Trade. Under the Light Railways Act of 1896, the Order when approved would have the effect of a private Act of Parliament, and it was still the custom, following 19th century practice, that it should not only give powers for the construction of the railway but also incorporate the company to which those powers were given. This procedure dated back to the days when companies of shareholders were very rare and privileged bodies, invariably incorporated by Royal Warrant or by special Act. It was not until the Limited Liability Act of 1855 that forming a company became a simple matter of registration under certain fixed rules. One of Howey's odder achievements was to bring about the formation of one of the very last companies, and certainly the last railway company, incorporated under that archaic procedure. But in drafting the Order the question arose, what should the new company be called? Logic would demand either a name relating to the area served (such as 'Romney Marsh Light Railway') or something specific (such as 'Hythe & New Romney' or 'New Romney, Dymchurch, & Hythe') with the place names given in their correct geographical order. Instead, many tedious hours spent scanning Latin verse at Eton had their possibly unconscious effect, and Howey chose 'Romney, Hythe & Dymchurch' because it sounded better. So it does, but it confuses some visitors to this day.

The public inquiry into the application for a Light Railway Order for the Romney, Hythe & Dymchurch Light Railway was held at New Romney on 15 and 16 January 1926, before the Light Railways Commissioner, none other than Mr Erskine. Howey and his friend J. A. Holder attended as Promoters of the scheme, and were represented by Mr A. Highmore King. Objectors each represented by Counsel were the East Kent Road Car Company, the Owners' and Occupiers' Association (a body hastily formed for the purpose), J. A. Heritage, Hythe Corporation, New Romney Corporation, and the Romney Marsh Rural District Council, though the last three bodies had only a watching brief, and were generally in favour.

Mr King started by making the case for the railway, which had the full support of the County Council, and called a number of witnesses. One of them was Major McConnell, licensee of the Ocean Inn at Dymchurch, who had chaired a number of public meetings and reported that the citizens of Dymchurch were strongly in favour of the railway. They felt they were being held to ransom by the bus company, which charged a fare of two shillings return for the five miles from Hythe, which was quite extortionate; competition was essential. The Commercial Manager of the Southern Railway, W. A. Brown, also gave evidence; there was no possibility of any standard gauge line, but the SR would improve the train service to New Romney, including putting on Sunday trains, if the RH&DR were built.

The fireworks started when Henry Greenly started to give technical evidence. He was able to silence suggestions that no 15in gauge line could be of any practical use by quoting his experience on the Eskdale, which was by now handling a considerable amount of stone traffic as well as a good passenger business, but he had to face much more difficult questions about his cost estimates. It was suggested that not only were these laughably inadequate, but his own figures gave the cost of the railway as only £44 less than the company's share capital. Even if all went well it could only start 'strangled at birth'. Indeed, the estimate he had put in for building the line was very meagre, allowing just for a single line with no passing places, only three locomotives, no workshops, and so on. Bombarded on all sides, he could only point out that he had already secured a quantity of rails at much under the price quoted by the objectors, and that the cost of building workshops was to be met by another company, Jackson Rigby Engineering, with which he was concerned and which proposed to bring its model engineering business down to New Romney.

Howey also had a rough passage. It was put to him that he was merely a hobbyist, causing an uproar to gratify a whim. There was nothing to

Nearly 50 years after being photographed alongside *Typhoon* at King's Cross shed, No. 4472 *Flying Scotsman*, by then the last survivor of Gresley's non-streamlined Pacifics, meets *Southern Maid* at Tyseley depot, Birmingham. (*G. A. Barlow*)

stop him getting bored with the railway and walking off, leaving it derelict. He answered that the shareholders were quite prepared to lose money, though he did not think they would. As to the objection that he might tire of the railway, he answered 'why should I get tired of it? I do not tire of things.' Two other significant exchanges were:

Counsel: 'I suppose if you fail to obtain this site you would be equally happy elsewhere?'

Howey: 'No, I would not be. We have found a site where the public evidently want a railway.'

Counsel: 'Are you going to give an undertaking you are going to provide this service, and hereafter you will endow it?'

Howey: 'Certainly not.'

The objectors then put their case. Alfred Boynton, Secretary of the East Kent Road Car Company, who had done most to orchestrate the opposition, came first. He dealt with the damaging evidence about his fares by promising to cut them during the 1926 season to 1s 3d (6p) return from Hythe to Dymchurch, others in proportion; these figures were still rather on the high side, and there was no way he could make this reduction look like anything other than the first benefit of the proposed railway. However, he soldiered on. The RH&DR would seriously injure business on the Folkestone to New Romney and Lydd service, which except in summer was a loser

anyhow. But the only worthwhile traffic on it were passengers going through to Folkestone, who would never use the railway. The buses had to obey a 12mph speed limit, the trains would probably run at up to 20, but the buses would still be faster. Mr King had little trouble tying him up in quite a satisfactory knot, and finally dispatched him with the comment that all the evidence about the railway's unprofitability was something purely for the promoters, who were after all not going to the public for money. It did not concern the inquiry at all.

Much more damaging was the expert witness put up by the EKRC, A. R. Hoare, a consulting engineer with considerable light railway and tramway experience. Except for *Green Goddess*, which he had inspected and admitted was a 'lovely machine', he could find nothing to be said for the scheme whatever. He considered the estimated cost of the railway, just under £25,000, at least £10,000 too low. The bridge at The Warren would cost £2,000, not £340. Fencing would cost £700 per mile, not £264. A minimum of five locomotives would be needed. Track would cost nearly 50 percent more than allowed for, and there would have to be passing loops. The cost quoted for locomotives and rolling stock was 'ridiculous'; if Greenly could build a four-wheeled goods wagon for £18, he would like to see it. The formation should be raised a couple of feet above the ground to allow for flooding and ensure a good foundation for the track. The terminus at Gallows Corner, half a mile short of the shops at Hythe, finally damned the proposal; the line would be useless except for joyriders.

Breaking ground across the Marsh: 1926 (*Henry Greenly*)

Manhandling the girders for the Duke of York's Bridge under the main road at The Warren; July 1926. (*A. L. S. Richardson*)

Next the landowners had their say. Their objections related mainly to the cutting-up of their land for a 'useless' railway. If there was to be a connection with the Dover–London line at Sandling, as had been intended in the earlier schemes, it might be different, but Greenly had agreed that the difference in levels made this quite impractical. Mr H. Rigden, the largest landowner on the Marsh, gave his opinion that no farmer would use the line for any purpose. For example, he sent his sheep away each winter by walking them the six or seven miles to Westenhanger station, on the Folkestone–Ashford main line. He

would never put them into little trucks to be taken to New Romney and then transhipped for a longer haul on the standard gauge. A number of individuals complained about losing their land's development value, but remarkably few could actually prove that any development on their land was actually intended. Mr Heritage, a farmer who objected to the railway on the grounds that it was a mere tramway running along the road, and presumably thought he was still objecting to the 1906 proposal for the Cinque Ports Electric Tramway, had gone so far as to retain Counsel. On the day of the inquiry, he had a possibly diplomatic cold and did not attend; his lawyer did the best he could with his brief. The developers of the Littlestone Estate, near New Romney, had spent a lot of money establishing it 'on the most select lines'; the railway 'would bring trippers to Littlestone and the present residents would pack up.' The Secretary of the Littlestone Golf Club said that the railway could not be permanent, and 'holidaymakers would not improve the amenities of the area. The railway would bring trippers of the paper bag and orange peel variety.' After a deal more of this sort of thing, the proceedings concluded and the Commissioner took the full size train back to London.

What went on at the Ministry in deciding the issue can only be surmised, but two things are clear. One is that the 1896 Light Railways Act placed the Commissioners under a duty to give every proper encouragement to promoters of Light Railways, which was a weight in the balance. The other was that ample funds were clearly available for the RH&DR; other than compensation, the only real objection to it had been that it might become abandoned and derelict, and there were precedents as to how that problem could be dealt with. It did not take the Minister long to make up his mind; on 19 February 1926 he gave notice that he intended to grant the Light Railway Order with certain protective clauses inserted, one of which was a provision that should the railway cease to operate for longer than 12 months, its lands might revert to their previous owners. The company's capital would also be increased from £25,000 to £33,000. On 26 May 1926 the Order was finally confirmed, and the RH&DR was officially in being.

During this last three month interval there was another clash with Mayor Luxmoor. Howey had been impatient, as always, to see progress made, and although New Romney station and workshops had been largely completed by May, and three miles of track laid in isolated lengths where landowners had been willing to sell early, there was a gap at The Warren. Here the line was to pass under the main road and then cross a plot of land which belonged to the New Romney Corporation, used as a rubbish dump and storage yard. At the end of February, after the Minister's preliminary notice of intention to grant the Order, Greenly told the Corporation he was sending in a gang of men to start digging. Mr Luxmoor hit the roof. Like an admiral on the bridge of a proud but torpedoed and sinking battleship, he continued to flare defiance; nothing could happen until the Order was signed and sealed, he said, and unless this trespass stopped immediately, legal action would follow. He was technically right, of course, though what the ratepayers would have said if he had carried out his threat is another matter. Anyhow, Greenly withdrew again until on 26 May the waters closed over the gallant Mayor's head.

3
Equipment and Extension

The early history of the RH&DR forms a picture of ambitious plans rapidly changed and discarded in favour of even more ambitious ones. It cannot really be said that Howey started by being cautious; a cautious man would never have started at all. But his vision and optimism widened in a series of leaps. The manner in which the locomotives were ordered makes a good illustration of this.

Reasonably enough, Howey waited until receiving word from the Ministry that they intended to grant the Light Railway Order before doing anything about enlarging the fleet beyond the two original Pacifics *Green Goddess* and *Northern Chief*, which would admittedly not have been enough. This clearance was received during February 1926. At once a third engine – to be named *Southern Maid* – was ordered from Paxmans, identical to the first two, and within a few days Greenly was discussing with Roland Martens, of the firm of Krauss in Munich, the question of a small shunting locomotive which would also be useful during construction work. This was ordered in March and delivered in August. A stock of four engines would have fulfilled Greenly's estimate, but by May Howey had decided to go much further. Shortly after the LRO was confirmed, he ordered another four from Paxmans, so that five were actually in production there simultaneously. This batch was to be closely similar in appearance to the three earlier machines, and to use as many as possible of the same parts, but its members differed considerably in detail.

The County Council had asked that facilities for ballast traffic be made available, so two engines were modified for freight working, with smaller driving wheels and a 4–8–2 wheel arrangement instead of 4–6–2. In keeping with their role they were named *Samson* and *Hercules*. The other two were to be Pacifics, but more powerful ones; like their main-line prototypes, they were to have three cylinders, each the same size as the two of the original engines. These two carried the names *Typhoon* and *Hurricane*. Howey took this decision before there had been any opportunity to try out in practice whether the third cylinder would be useful or whether enough steam could be made to furnish and enough adhesion weight existed to use a 50 per cent increase in tractive effort; he just liked the idea. In fact it proved a failure on the whole. On a good day with a clean fire the three-cylinder engines could go like the wind, but they were correspondingly heavier on fuel and water at all times, and certainly there was something radically wrong with Greenly's inside valve gear, a radial type of his own design, almost inaccessibly located between the frames; for all its faults, the external derived valve gear Gresley used to drive the middle cylinder on his own engines would have made a vastly better job. Following a series of troubles, *Typhoon*'s centre cylinder was taken out of use and the driving wheels requartered in 1935. *Hurricane*, as she was Howey's own engine, remained as she was, and he got round the water problem by fitting her with a new high-capacity tender in 1934. Then one day in July 1937 the inside gear locked solid in the middle of the Marsh while she was working a well-filled train towards Hythe, tying up the service for some hours. Howey had been warned the day before that trouble was brewing and that the engine should not be used, but for some reason it was. This embarrassment brought about the end of three-cylinder propulsion, and shortly

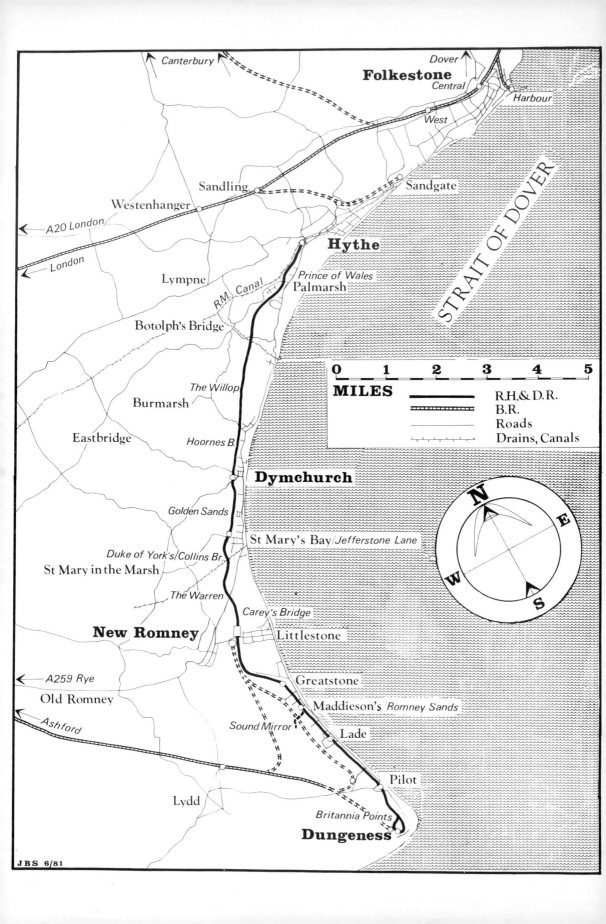

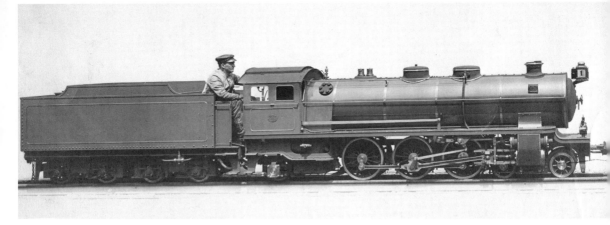

Greenly's rival; a works photograph of one of the 15in gauge Pacifics designed for Krauss of Munich by Roland Martens.

afterward he had his revenge on the engine by renaming her *Bluebottle*, though he relented after 1945.

The Krauss locomotive was a much simpler proposition. It was to be a version, cut down in height and modified to suit the gauge, of the smallest of the firm's standard industrial locomotives, the 10/12hp 2ft gauge 0–4–0T. Aside from the obvious alteration to frame and wheels, Martens listed the other changes in a letter to Greenly dated 25 February 1926. A tender was to be added; the boiler was to be lowered 2in; the back end of the frame was to be shortened to allow for the fact that the driver would occupy the tender and not the cab; the smokebox would be 2in longer; and the chimney, cab, and dome lowered. None of these alterations was very radical. It was not possible to reduce overall height below 5ft 0½in, although Greenly had asked for 4ft 7in to compare with the Paxman engines and a scale one-third of the British loading gauge. But this did not really matter since the coaches were going to be higher than this anyhow. It was suggested that the tender might be built locally to save expense, but even without this a price of £260 for delivery at Munich compared very favourably with £1,250 or more for each of the Paxman engines. Nor did Krauss do badly with this modified type; shortly afterwards they built two more, identical, for a railway in a Munich park.

Martens had earlier submitted a proposal to build some of the standard Krauss 15in gauge Pacifics, which he had designed, for the RH&DR. A first batch of three of these was already under construction in 1926 for a proposed line in

Dresden, where they are still operating, and others were later built for Vienna, Stuttgart, Seville, New Delhi, and other cities, no fewer than 15 being turned out by 1950. But Howey decided firmly against the idea. Greenly and Martens were friends of long standing, but Howey had very little use for things German and insisted on calling the Krauss 0–4–0 *The Bug*. Possibly one school of thought is right in saying that this name was a natural and proper choice for any Gentleman's Light Sports Locomotive, like the Bugatti Gentleman's Light Sports Car of the day, and Howey certainly once remarked that *The Bug* and a Bugatti had similar riding qualities, or lack of them. But the majority view has always been that Howey chose the name for its beetle-like connotations and always had insecticide at the back of his mind.

Thus the complete list of numbers and names for the original locomotive fleet was:

No 1	4–6–2	*Green Goddess*	
No 2	4–6–2	*Northern Chief*	
No 3	4–6–2	*Southern Maid*	
No 4	0–4–0TT	*The Bug*	
No 5	4–8–2	*Hercules*	
No 6	4–8–2	*Samson*	
No 7	4–6–2	*Typhoon*	(3-cylinder)
No 8	4–6–2	*Hurricane*	(3-cylinder)

It is interesting to note that all these names except perhaps the first are rather grandiose and delightfully unsuitable for miniature locomotives. *Southern Maid* was an obvious match for *Northern Chief*, but was in fact originally intended to be *Southern Chief*. *Green Goddess* is slightly out of keeping with all the others, and the author has always supposed that this, as the first locomotive of all, was the one Zborowski had intended for himself and that he had chosen the name before he died. Howey always said that the name was suggested by the successful play of the early 1920s, *The Green Goddess*, which starred George Arliss and involved early escapades with aeroplanes in India; but Zborowski was just as interested in the theatre and had indeed married an actress. The truth can never be known now. The missing number 4 was allocated to *The Bug*, which fell into this place by reason of the date it was ordered.

If Greenly, with Howey and Zborowski standing behind him, reached the summit of his achievement with these locomotives, the rolling stock he produced for the RH&DR was much less satisfactory. He made the mistake of deciding to use four-wheeled coaches, based on Bassett-Lowke's standard pre first world war light garden railway open coaches with a candy-striped canvas awning roof, several of which had been running for some time at Ravenglass. Greenly realised that better bodies were needed, and went to a great deal of trouble to develop a vehicle with a very low centre of gravity which would not blow over in the perennial Marsh gales. By 1928 no fewer than 117 four-wheelers had been built, in two batches, one open-sided and one with mica side-screens between the doors. All sat eight passengers in two four-seat compartments, except for five vehicles modified as guard's and luggage vans. But they rode appallingly badly at Romney speeds. Greenly had not appreciated how different things were at 25mph compared with 15mph or so at Sand Hutton or Staughton Manor. They were a serious disappointment.

Something much better was going to be needed if the railway was to have any hope of attracting passengers during the winter. During 1927 Greenly therefore designed eight closed coaches which, in total contrast, were probably the best 15in gauge passenger stock ever built. As delivered by the Clayton Wagon Company in 1928, they were 12-seat bogie vehicles, with three four-seat compartments and two small luggage compartments, one at each end. They closely resembled main-line stock, with hinged doors, droplight windows, electric light, and steam heat. This last was particularly effective. Young Terry Holder was on the train when it was first tried out. The coaches had just been varnished and the windows, as it happened, were all stuck shut. Howey drove, and in his usual full-throttle style turned up the pressure on the steam heat line to maximum on leaving New Romney. The compartments slowly got more and more like the hot room in a sauna bath; when the train got to

Hythe the windows were all misted up and the customers were bright red and gasping. Social conventions in the 1920s were still so strong that none of them had removed any clothes. Modifications followed. Unfortunately these coaches were supplied on complex bogies of Greenly's design which were not satisfactory, and although they rode better than the four-wheelers the improvement was not very great.

About half the four-wheeled coaches were fitted with the vacuum brake complete, the remaining vehicles carrying through brake pipes only. The Vacuum Brake Company designed special small-sized cylinders and ejectors to suit. This equipment has stood the test of time and is still in use, though now nearly every coach is fully fitted. *Green Goddess* had originally been fitted with the Westinghouse compressed air brake as well, probably at Zborowski's request, but this was removed in 1927, and no Romney coaches ever had this brake. Unfortunately the fact that only some of the original coaches had working brakes, and they were difficult to distinguish from the others that were only piped, meant that the actual braking power of any particular train set, assembled at random, was quite unpredictable. And since most locomotive brakes were pretty poor, drivers had some hairy moments and tended to approach stations, Hythe with its fixed buffers in particular, showing a marked lack of confidence.

For freight traffic there were a considerable number of Heywood-type small four-wheeled wagons, with planked floor and low sides which could be lifted bodily off the frames. Some of these simple affairs, which might well have cost as little as the £18 Greenly estimated, were supplied by Theakstons; other were built at New Romney by Jackson, Rigby. After the construction period they were used mainly for coal or for ballast. A few were later given much more conventional wooden wagon bodies with side doors. The sheep traffic which Greenly had originally hoped for, and in due course the almost equally non-existent fish traffic from Dungeness, was to be carried in two long open-topped bogie wagons built by Jackson, Rigby; in fact these proved quite useful for handling passengers' luggage and milk churns, etc, to the holiday camps. Much the most impressive wagons were six purchased second-hand from Eskdale in 1929. These were 6-ton capacity steel-bodied bogie vehicles with bottom hopper doors, which Howey acquired in case the prospect of ballast traffic from West Hythe should come to anything. It never did, but they were still

Dymchurch station before the line was opened. *Southern Maid* on a test run to Hythe; Howey standing next to the engine, accompanied by the current railway dog. Note Greenly's economical combined double Gents' and footbridge.

quite useful in the reballasting programme carried out during the 1930s, which consisted mainly in applying a thin top-dressing of crushed rock in conspicuous places near bridges and level crossings.

Another example of the way Howey's plans gradually became larger was in the matter of double track. Greenly's original proposal had been to build a single line throughout, although the Light Railway Order gave power to add a second track. During the summer of 1926, when New Romney station was opened to visitors even though no trains were running, Howey was heartened by the number of people taking an interest and as well as ordering more engines told Greenly he wanted a double track as far as Dymchurch. This made some sense, since it was then expected that the main traffic would come from the SR connections at New Romney and that many passengers would only go as far as Dymchurch, where the station was originally laid out with bay platforms and turntable to enable trains from New Romney to be reversed easily. But by the time tracklaying had actually reached Dymchurch, Howey had decided to go the whole hog and put in double track all the way to Hythe.

Due to the delay in starting work on the bridge at The Warren, the original hope of opening the line as far as Dymchurch during the 1926 season was frustrated. Instead, construction was carried out at a fairly deliberate pace, aiming at opening

for the summer holiday season of 1927. But during 1926 there was one massive piece of favourable publicity. On 6 August the Duke of York (later King George VI), who was patron of a boys' camp next to the line, paid a visit. At that time one track had just been laid up to and across the bridge near the camp, and the event turned into a considerable party. The Duke travelled with Howey on *Northern Chief* for nearly two miles to New Romney, with Nigel Gresley, Chief Mechanical Engineer of the London & North Eastern Railway, sitting cross-legged on the back of the tender. A great number of people of lesser importance came too, and press cameras were out in force. At New Romney Howey showed the Duke round the station and works, and then they all went back again on the train. As a promotion the event could not have been faulted, and the photographs were in most papers the next day. The RH&DR is perhaps the only railway whose first train was a royal one.

But one jarring note was struck which was not publicised. Although Greenly was seldom more than a few feet away from him during the visit, Howey for one reason or another never presented him to the Duke, which was to say the least insensitive of him. Greenly was a proud and touchy man, and was quite shattered by this apparent snub. It is not too much to say that relations between him and Howey were never quite the same again; the old cheerful spirit of joint enterprise went, and was replaced by something more doubtful. Many people commented that Greenly only recovered his old high spirits during Howey's absence, which were still quite frequent, particularly his annual visit to

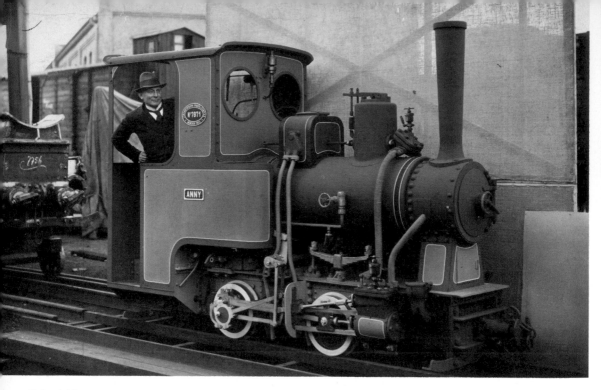

Roland Martens on the footplate of one of the standard Krauss 0–4–0Ts which he proposed to alter to 15in gauge; the photograph he sent to Henry Greenly to illustrate the idea which formed the basis of *The Bug*.

Australia.

In matters where Howey took little interest, Greenly built the line in accordance with his estimates; in other words, very cheaply indeed. The railway's buildings, which he designed, were on the whole pretty gimcrack and jerrybuilt, although this was not so noticeable since some of the housing development taking place in the area at the time was of very much the same kind. The bridges carrying the line over the drainage channels in the Marsh were none too substantial, and were designed for a fairly limited life. The two bridges carrying roads over, fortunately, were much better. One of them, near the Prince of Wales Inn, still stands; the other, at The Warren, was rebuilt by the County Council in 1973 only because it would have to carry the occasional 350-ton special heavy load to and from the nuclear power stations at Dungeness.

The opposition at the inquiry had sworn that good, substantial fences could hardly be put up for three times the price that Greenly had estimated, and they were probably right. Certainly the original fences were very poor. The railway was sued in November 1930 for the value of a mare which got onto the line near the Prince of Wales and had to be destroyed after being struck by a train. Evidence was given that the wires were much too low; indeed one witness said he had seen a cow jump onto the line. The railway had to pay £60 plus costs.

A much more successful economy was in buying rail. The opposition had given a much higher price to the inquiry and lost ground when Greenly proved them wrong; but the explanation was simply that the rail he bought was second-hand. During the first world war an enormous mileage of temporary 2ft gauge railways had been laid down behind the lines by both sides, to bring up supplies to the trenches. By the mid-1920s nearly all these tracks had been lifted and Greenly had been able to buy a large amount of nearly new rail very cheaply. Curiously enough, it came from both sides. The British and French had used mainly 25 lb/yard rail of standard American section, considerable tonnages of which were imported, while the Germans used a very similar 12kg/metre rail of Belgian standard section, produced by steelworks at that time under their control. The two sections could not really be mixed, but it took a very careful examination to tell one from the other. The main difference was that they needed different sizes of fishplate to make a satisfactory joint. Greenly obtained this material through the firm of Francis Theakston Ltd, which had a workshop in Crewe; Colonel Theakston took a close personal interest in the RH&DR and ultimately did a lot of its purchasing and specification work. His firm certainly did a first class job in making the RH&DR points and

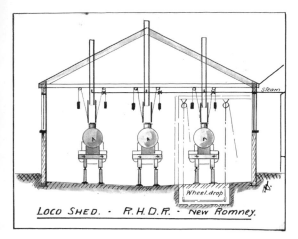

LOCO SHED. · R.H.D.R. · New Romney.

Greenly's original proposal for the locomotive shed at New Romney. Having the track raised on stilts was a radical improvement but Howey unfortunately did not agree to the almost ideal, but expensive, arrangement of counterbalanced extension chimneys (used at Ravenglass), shown here with the added refinement of steam-induced forced draught. Until a version of these extension chimneys was installed in 1976, the shed at night, with six or more engines cooling down, became a cross between a Turkish Bath and a gas chamber.

crossings, which were to a very high standard.

The original New Romney station, of which only a part survives, was a terminus which faced across Littlestone Road to the SR station. Entry to the four platforms was through the booking office building which still serves that purpose, approached by a drive-in crescent for cars and taxis, just like a London terminus. The faint resemblance to King's Cross was struck again by a miniature clock tower, though until 1978 only the face towards the railway actually held a clock. The platforms were laid out to suit main-line methods of working; two tracks were set for arriving trains, and connected at the buffers to allow the engine to escape provided its train was quite short – not more than about 130ft long. The other two platforms could only be conveniently used for departures. It was clearly intended that a second locomotive should be available to switch incoming coaches from one track to another while the engine which brought them in went off to be turned and serviced. The absurd wastefulness of this (even at King's Cross, where admittedly lack of space prevented more economical working) was disregarded.

Just beyond the signalbox which controlled the exit from the platforms stood the workshops area, with buildings on each side of the main line. To the east was the three-road locomotive shed, approached across a turntable. Next door was an equally large workshop, occupied by Jackson Rigby & Co Ltd, with shared staff room and toilet block connecting the two buildings. Behind the locomotive shed was a small carpenter's shop, reached by another siding. On the west side of the main line stood two carriage sheds, and beyond them a 15in gauge track ran up to and along the full length of a 250ft platform, whose other face was occupied by the standard gauge siding whose level crossing with Littlestone Road had caused such a fuss. This platform was intended for the work of transhipping freight between the two railways; for the security of valuables there was a small lock-up goods shed entered by the 15in gauge. Just to the east of the engine shed and works Howey had erected for his family a large and comfortable bungalow which he named *Red Tiles*, and which Greenly had designed as well as the other buildings; a little further along and on the other side of the tracks Greenly had built a small bungalow for himself.

There was no reason why the main line should not have gone straight as an arrow out of the station, but it did not. With a showman's instinct Greenly had thought it would produce a greater impression if, instead of appearing as a slowly approaching pinhead in the distance, an arriving train should burst out suddenly between the buildings. For this reason the engine shed and workshops were sited so as to block the view from the platforms, and the main line left between them by means of a sharp S-bend. Once clear, however, it straightened out, and for the rest of the way to Hythe there were no curves unless they were required either to give a better angle of approach to bridges or to avoid coming too close to buildings or other obstructions, which included following close to boundaries of land as much as possible to avoid problems of severance.

For practically the whole way to Hythe the railway in 1927 ran through green fields. The only houses it passed near were a few at St Mary's Bay, most surviving from the wartime Royal Flying Corps establishment and occupied by the Boys' Camp; and on the outskirts of Dymchurch village, where the station was very much at the fringe of things. There were also a few near Burmarsh Road and the Prince of Wales. Although the land looks quite flat, it is not so in truth, and there are some noticeable though fairly easy gradients. The main coast road at The Warren follows the crest of a low sandy ridge

New Romney station and works were tolerably complete for the summer of 1926, allowing that part of the railway to be on show even while the rest was under construction. On the day of the Duke of York's visit, *Northern Chief* (Nigel Gresley in the cab) waits at the head of the first six coaches to be delivered, with Howey and Greenly standing on the platform.

which once formed the shoreline on the north side of Romney Haven. The line climbs slowly towards it across the old harbour bed from New Romney station, to pass under the road bridge, a mile from

New Romney locomotive shed, with *Northern Chief* on the turntable and a considerable crowd of VIPs, including the Duke of York, Howey, Nigel Gresley, and Greenly.

the start, through a shallow cutting which tends to attract snowdrifts in hard winters, then falls again towards St Mary's Bay station, 2¼ miles from New Romney. There is another noticeable rise and fall between there and Dymchurch, and a short sharp rise half a mile beyond; the rest of the way to Hythe, except for a pronounced dip under the Prince of Wales bridge, is fairly level.

During the mid 1920s there had been some manoeuvring going on about place names at St Mary's Bay, which had until then been known as Jesson, with the road called Jesson Lane and the RFC camp Jesson Camp. As the land began to be built over, the developers thought this name rather undistinguished, and wanted something which sounded more attractive and evocative of the seaside. In due course they had their way and

the locality, with the station, was officially renamed. At the same time the road was promoted to Jefferstone Lane, echoing H. G. Wells's account of how a social climber named Snooks became Mr Sevenoaks. Anyhow, Jesson station was, and St Mary's Bay station is, a very simple affair, with two platforms, one shelter and one office hut. Originally there were some signals worked from a lever frame in the booking office. There was at the outset talk of putting in a siding for goods traffic consigned to the local coal merchant (who had said he would use the railway) and the boys' camp, but this was never done, though some coal seems to have been carried all the same in the early years. The nearby airfield remained in occasional use, as a diversionary ground from Lympne airport, until 1945 when it was superseded by the second world war airfield at Lydd.

Dymchurch station, $3\frac{1}{4}$ miles from New Romney, originally called Dymchurch (Marshlands), was a much bigger affair, boasting a rather small overall roof looking as if it had been extracted from one of the middle-range Hornby train sets, as well as a separate booking office building and a signalbox. A tea room was soon added, but converted before long into a small cottage. Greenly hit on a useful economy in using each gents' toilet as the support for the footbridge. The bay platforms and turntable originally provided saw little use, particularly as they faced New Romney and it was soon found that when trains did require to be turned at Dymchurch, they came from Hythe. A second crossover was put in at the Hythe end of the station to deal with these, and the rest gradually removed, except for one siding which survives.

Apart from these two main intermediate stations, there were originally others. A halt was briefly tried at The Warren. There was a similarly abortive one at the Prince of Wales Bridge, which seems never to have been used at all. Much longer-lived was Burmarsh Road ($4\frac{1}{4}$ miles from New Romney), which served the north end of Dymchurch village and any villager of Burmarsh who was prepared to walk $1\frac{1}{2}$ miles to reach it. This station was originally equipped similarly to St Mary's Bay, but was closed to regular traffic and demolished before 1939. A couple of miles further on, across a wide stretch of open marshland known as The Willop and next to the level crossing with Botolph's Bridge Road (6 miles from New Romney) stood Botolph's Bridge Halt, complete with a small wooden shelter. Since even now there is hardly a house to be seen in any

direction from here, it is surprising that this station survived at all, but it did not survive for long. One summer evening in the 1930s Howey decided to close it down, and summarily did so with a tin of petrol and a box of matches. Gratifying though the blaze was, some passer-by spoilt the fun by calling the fire brigade and the police, who were not amused.

Finally, $8\frac{1}{4}$ miles from New Romney, the line reached Hythe station, situated at Gallows Corner on Scanlons Bridge Road and, just as Mr Hoare had pointed out at the inquiry, $\frac{1}{2}$-mile short of the shops in the High Street. Here, in 1927, there was a fairly simple station, with a roof over four platforms, signalbox, turntable, small engine shed, and a siding for goods traffic which led out into the station car park. For the last mile the line had followed quite closely to the Royal Military Canal, and Greenly laid out the terminus so as to allow room for a quite large and attractive restaurant and cafeteria building between the platforms and the towpath. Unfortunately while this was being put up Howey, bored with the idea of selling cups of tea, sold the property off freehold to somebody with a bit of commercial judgment. There was also a small bungalow on the opposite side of the station, intended for the stationmaster/superintendent and for a time occupied by him, but sold in 1947.

Scenically, the attractions of the lineside country can perhaps be described as low key. There is a pleasant view of the chalk escarpment which marks the northern edge of Romney Marsh and which further east becomes the Dover cliffs; the line draws close to this beyond Botolph's Bridge, and by the time it reaches the canal runs at the very foot of the hills. The ruins of the old Roman fort of Portus Lemanis can still be plainly seen from the train. Excitement of another kind has always been provided by the skeletal and parapetless bridges over the drainage cuts, particularly the largest of them. This spans 60ft, a distance rather too great to be conveniently got over by Greenly's usual method of flinging down a few girders, pouring concrete round their ends, and laying rails and sleepers on top. Howey in any case decided to have one bridge on his railway that looked like a proper railway bridge, and Colonel Theakston was commissioned to manufacture a twin through truss steel girder bridge, brought in sections by rail to the site. Since this was the bridge which featured in the Duke of York's visit, it was thereafter named in his honour. It may not have been parapetless, but it was still thrilling since it drummed and rattled

The Duke of York drives *Northern Chief* out of New Romney station with the first passenger train; Howey also on the footplate, Gresley sitting on the back of the tender, and wagons coupled behind the six coaches to take the overflow crowd.

under the train in a thoroughly full-sized manner.

The official opening of the railway took place on Saturday 16 July 1927, with Earl Beauchamp KG, Lord Warden of the Cinque Ports, clearing the starting signal at Hythe to allow a long train

of guests and dignitaries, headed by *Hercules*, to leave. This was nicely in time for the peak holiday traffic as well. The public were well aware of the connection Howey and his friends had with

The Official Opening, 16 July 1927. Earl Beauchamp (Lord Warden of the Cinque Ports) carrying his souvenir guidebook, inspects *Hercules*; followed by General Sir Ivor Maxse (Chairman of the RH&D Light Railway Company) and Howey in top hats, and flanked by Robert Hardie, RH&DR Traffic Manager.

Brooklands, and Brooklands people and motor racing in general were, in those pre-pop, pre-television days, star attractions. There was plenty of publicity, and crowds descended on the railway. Early photographs show packed trains with happy throngs on the platforms waiting for the next one. Everything ran smoothly and there were no hitches, except for a most unfortunate one on 17 August when Harold Adams, a 27-year-old platelayer, stepped out of the way of one train near the Prince of Wales bridge straight into the path of another, and was killed. Yet even this demonstrated that the RH&DR was something to be taken seriously.

Meanwhile, Howey had begun to think about extending the line to Dungeness. This would give it five more miles of route, of quite a different character. At that time no road went further south than Littlestone; beyond lay a long stretch of bare shingle beach, with the occasional fisherman's/smuggler's hut, the coastguard cottages at Lade, and little else until the lighthouse and lifeboat station at the tip of the point. The map showed footpaths, but to walk on these and on the shingle in any comfort the locals wore shoes reminiscent of Clementine's Herring Boxes Without Topses. Dungeness was already served by the SR branch from Lydd, but although the New Romney passenger train went down there when it had nothing better to do, the real purpose of that line was to bring out shingle ballast The whole area around Dungeness, in fact, had for many years belonged to the old South Eastern Railway, whose whole system was ballasted with Dungeness 'beach'. For a standard gauge railway, this made a most unsatisfactory trackbed, since it consists wholly of low-grade ball bearings, but then the South Eastern was a rather unsatisfactory railway so nobody noticed. The Southern was trying to improve matters following its formation in 1923; in its efforts to do so it brought bigger locomotives and faster trains into Kent, and was rewarded by the major derailment of a Folkestone and Dover express near Sevenoaks on 24 August 1927. This very nasty smash was fundamentally caused by the use of shingle ballast, but it was some time before this became clear as there was an immediate scare about the use of the River class 2–6–4 tank engines, one of which was involved, on fast trains. So it was still officially SR policy to excavate the Dungeness area for shingle.

For most of the way the RH&DR extension would therefore have the place to itself, and there were in fact no objections made to the Light Railway Order. The second Public Inquiry, held at New Romney on 18 April 1928, was a pushover compared to the first. The Board of Trade approved of better access being available to three miles of beach in case of emergency, and sent somebody down from London to say so; the Coastguard service was delighted that its men would no longer have to walk over four miles of shingle to Lydd or Littlestone, the County looked forward to better times for the fishermen of Dungeness with better transport. The Romney, Hythe & Dymchurch Light Railway (Extension) Order was therefore confirmed on 12 July 1928. This was just as well, since the line had already been opened as far as The Pilot (4 miles from New Romney) on 24 May. As Mayor Luxmoor had discovered, Howey did not like waiting for starter's orders.

The major constructional problem on the Dungeness extension was in fact at New Romney. Part of the brand-new station had to be torn to pieces to allow the double track of the extension to drop into a cutting and pass under the road through another of Greenly's reinforced concrete twin arch bridges. Here the tracks were for much of the time below the level of the water table, and had to be pumped dry; the site was also very constricted. It was just possible to get past the SR station area by using retaining walls and a narrow cutting, but there was no room for two new platforms anywhere. The answer to this problem was at first the awkward one of providing a new southbound platform at a lower level in the original station (replacing two of the original four) and a new northbound platform, complete with its own waiting room and footbridge, some distance away on the south side of Littlestone Road and close to the SR station.

Beyond here, the new line climbed steadily alongside the SR tracks until, after half a mile, it reached the old sea wall which had marked the south side of the mediaeval harbour, and curved round to run along the top of it towards the coast. At Greatstone (originally Greatstone Dunes, $1\frac{1}{4}$ miles) a fairly large station was planned to serve an area where housing development was just beginning, and which the coast road had just been extended to serve. There followed a quarter-mile climb at 1 in 120, perhaps the most noticeable gradient on the railway, to the crest of the shingle bank at the head of the beach, which it followed for the rest of the way. Originally there were small halts only at Lade ($2\frac{3}{4}$ miles), for the coastguard cottages, and The Pilot Inn ($4\frac{1}{4}$ miles) where a rather larger station building was provided

Hercules leaves Hythe with the inaugural train, 16 July 1927.

together with a triangle for turning locomotives during the few months that this was the terminus. Maddieson's Camp (2 miles) was added when the holiday camp was opened during the 1930s.

The last section to Dungeness ($5\frac{1}{2}$ miles from New Romney), opened at the beginning of August 1928, involved some rather heavier construction work, since the shingle had in places been heaped up by ancient storms into ridges and valleys which the line had to cut and bank across. Greenly resolved to lay out Dungeness station not as a

The original New Romney terminus in 1927, before work started on the Dungeness extension; *Green Goddess* about to leave with a typically lightweight train.

terminus, but as a through station on a large circle, which formed the means of reversing the trains. He also designed a restaurant and cafe building, with flat over, near the station, as at Hythe; whether due to Greenly's persuasion or the lack of a businessman sufficiently acute to make an offer, Howey did not sell the structure and so the railway went unwillingly into the business of making cups of tea. All the way from The Pilot the line had been built on land belonging to the Southern Railway, who still intended to dig it out for ballast; for this reason the unusual arrangement was made that the SR would grant the RH&DR a right in perpetuity to lay and use a railway on its land, without any transfer of ownership, thus making it a simple legal matter to move the 15in gauge track if the SR should wish to dig under it.

Green Goddess entering Burmarsh Road station from Hythe in summer 1927. (*W. H. Whitworth*)

Since 1928 the railway's surroundings have changed more radically between Greatstone and Dungeness than anywhere else. What had been an uninterrupted view of the sea has now been blocked for much of the way by houses, and where there had originally been no level crossings with motorable roads there are now eight. Howey got one developer to erect a bridge to carry one new road, but had earlier allowed them to cross the track without question. A second bridge, near The Pilot, followed as part of a deal in which, to allow houses to be built on the strip of land between the railway and the new Coast Drive during the 1930s, the tracks were diverted some yards further inland. So the old open coastline has disappeared. Beyond The Pilot the scene changes to some extent; the SR sold its Dungeness Estate after 1945 and the new owners have allowed no new building, although there is of course the conspicuous exception of a pair of nuclear power stations. Nevertheless, some of the old unique flavour of Dungeness remains, windswept and end-of-the-worldly. Old wooden houses are scattered about still, which on close examination usually turn out to be built round discarded main line railway carriages, and the old close-knit fishing community still lives in them.

One of the 4–8–2s entering New Romney on the original curved alignment, shortly after opening. Straightening the track a couple of years later meant demolishing the three workshop buildings shown; only the locomotive shed survived.

4
The First Twelve Years

The 1926 Light Railway Order had appointed five people as original directors of the Romney, Hythe & Dymchurch Light Railway Company, Howey and his wife, two of his friends, Captain J. A. Holder and Major W. B. Bell, and Henry Greenly. The maximum number of directors was also set at five, and each would have to own at least 250 shares in the company. Greenly, however, never acquired more than 50 shares, and so was never qualified to sit on the Board; for the same reason Holder did not do so until 1929. Instead, by mid-1927 the two vacancies had been filled by K. Lee Guinness and A. J. J. Lucas, Howey's agent in Melbourne. In addition, Howey felt that the railway should have a prominent public figure as Chairman, and so Mrs Howey stood down and was replaced by General Sir Ivor Maxse, KCB, CVO, DSO.

Since Howey owned nearly all the shares in the company, and took a close personal interest in the railway, the Board did not have a very large

function and the Minute Book shows that its business was pretty well confined to approving contracts and appointments. No record survives of meetings earlier than July 1927, but on 6 July that year the Board formally appointed B. D. Bellamy General Manager and Secretary (at £35 a month), Greenly as Chief Engineer (at £33 6s 8d a month), Robert Hardie Traffic Manager at £5 a week, and A. G. Chaldecott (Jackson, Rigby's Manager), Works Manager at a rate to be agreed. At the same meeting, it was resolved that the RH&DR should take over the Jackson, Rigby business outright; evidently the inconvenience of having two separate companies occupying the same property had already begun to cause problems, although the takeover was not actually completed until the end of 1929.

With the railway completed, Henry Greenly was able to devote rather less time to its affairs. The Jackson, Rigby Engineering Co Ltd had just moved its workshops from Shalford in Surrey and was firmly established at New Romney, with a staff of a dozen men; apart from carrying out the RH&DR running repairs under its contract and producing its range of models and parts, it had recently built two 12in gauge 4–6–2s of

Driving the last spike at Dungeness. Greenly's old track gauge, in the foreground, remained in use for the next 50 years. Note the Heywood-type wagons, whose sides could be lifted off bodily to save the cost of doors, being used for ballast.

Samson did a little work in the first year or two and was then withdrawn from service; by 1939 it was a rusty hulk, raided for spare parts. This is a rare view of the engine at work in 1927, at Hythe. (*Locomotive Publishing Co*)

Greenly's design to the order of the Canadian Pacific Railway, which was to operate a line at the Exhibition in Philadelphia commemorating the 150th anniversary of the American Declaration of Independence.

But troubles were beginning to accumulate. Greenly had always insisted on his position as an independent professional, and although he took a salary from the RH&DR seems not to have accepted that this put him under any obligation to the Company. This finally caused a major row.

With the opening of the Dungeness extension, Howey decided that two more engines would be needed and placed an order for them with Paxmans. Shortly afterwards, however, he was persuaded by Greenly, and also by the experience of the first winter's running on the windswept marsh, that all the existing locomotives had a severe disadvantage. Built, even as overscale models, to a restricted British profile, their cabs were too small to offer their drivers much protection against the weather. This problem would be got over by building a similarly overscale engine not of a British prototype but of an American one. The much larger transatlantic profile would bring the cab up to a size which could offer some real protection. Howey accepted this case, cancelled the Paxmans order, and decided to have the engines built at New Romney. Paxmans provided the wheel and cylinder castings, which had already been made. Krauss were to provide the boilers, and Howey visited Munich to discuss them with Martens. The question was therefore one of designing a North American 4–6–2 round these parts, and Greenly's 12in gauge CPR design would serve as a useful model. Chaldecott gave A. L. S. Richardson,

Jackson Rigby's draughtsman, the task of working it all out, and at that point, in autumn 1928, Howey departed for Australia, travelling as he always did at that time via Canada, where the Canadian Pacific gave him a pass to ride on the footplate for as much of the transcontinental journey as he liked.

Richardson beavered away at a general arrangement and other drawings for the new engines, working from Greenly's earlier design and a photograph of CPR 4–6–2 No 2300. Meanwhile, Greenly and Bellamy had developed a fairly strong dislike for each other which grew unchecked in the Captain's absence. Bellamy was a young man, no technician, and Greenly evidently resented the fact that he was in a superior position. One straw in the wind was that at the end of September Greenly wrote again to Felix Pole at Paddington, on RH&DR paper, trying once more to get his agreement to the Brean Sands railway project, this time with Sir Aubrey Brocklebank as a backer.

By late January 1929 Richardson had more or less finished the drawings when Greenly went into the office one evening, took them away, and burned them. Not surprisingly, all hell broke loose. Bellamy called in the police, and Greenly was arrested and driven off to Lydd, but before going (according to a letter he wrote to his daughter) told Chaldecott 'that I had every right to go into the office from which the drawings were missed; that some of them were my personal property, and that the drawing of which they were particularly proud, and were searching for, was a copy of mine, and done without my permission.' This quotation gives us a pretty clear insight into the truth of the matter. However, whatever complaint he may have had, Greenly had clearly gone much too far, and it is hard not to sympathise with Bellamy's drastic action. The only trouble was, nothing could be proved in legal terms. The prosecution had to be withdrawn. Greenly had made the railway look vindictive,

Southern Maid enters Hythe in 1930, with three Clayton Pullmans in their original state and one four-wheeler. The need for luggage accommodation had been overlooked at first; note the bicycle loaded on the back of the tender. Prams and pushchairs were also carried in this manner, but they tended not to fit under the bridges, and the railway was constantly having to buy replacements. (*H. C. Casserley*)

and had to be compensated. Early in March 1929 he left New Romney, never to return, before Howey came back from Australia.

The sudden disappearance in such dramatic circumstances of one of its prime movers caused a considerable sensation on the railway, but things soon settled down. Bellamy, who seems to have been a charming lightweight, also left the scene during 1929. Chaldecott did his best loyally but his interest was in the model engineering side of the Jackson, Rigby business; in the aftermath of the scandal Howey decided that he did not wish this to be carried on at New Romney at all, and by the autumn of 1930 arrangements had been made for Chaldecott to take the patterns, equipment, and goodwill away to Brighton, where he set up independently. In practice, the responsibility for day-to-day running on the railway came to rest on Robert Hardie, the Traffic Manager, who lived in the station house at Hythe and held the position until the end of the 1937 season; he died in December of that year.

Bob Hardie was a much respected local character, who had been something of a rolling

Terry Holder, driving *Typhoon* in its three-cylinder condition, at Dymchurch with a down train, demonstrating the engine's inability to pass a water column. (*J. T. Holder*)

stone in his youth; he was very proud of having won the World Championship for Quick Shaving in Chicago in 1903–04. He had been one of Proctor Mitchell's associates in the travel trade before 1914, and had gone with him to Ravenglass in 1916; he was effectively the running foreman of the Ravenglass & Eskdale. Howey poached him away during 1926 to do the same job on the RH&DR, where he made himself equally indispensable.

Among the directors, Lucas, since he lived in Australia, left the scene fairly quickly, and never appears to have attended a meeting after the railway was opened. General Maxse had never intended to stay beyond an initial period, and resigned in October 1929, Howey succeeding him as Chairman. Mrs Howey then returned to the Board as Secretary and Director, and the other vacancy was taken up by Captain J. A. Holder. Holder had in fact been the major force behind, and shareholder in, the Jackson Rigby business, and had evidently tried to keep the peace over Greenly. Lee Guinness was not a fit man, never having really recovered from a serious motor racing smash in 1924; he died in 1937. By 1931 he had left the Board, as had Bell, and in February 1932 Holder's son Terence was appointed a director. For the rest of the decade the Minute Book records the two Howeys and the two Holders as governing the railway, with Hardie putting in a regular appearance at the AGM as the only attending shareholder. Apart from an occasional meeting with Mr Thomas, the railway's Accountant, no other person appears in the record. How many of the recorded meetings actually took place is another question, best left on the file next to the related question of how genuine were the figures in the statutory Traffic Returns submitted annually to the Ministry of Transport; Howey made sure they looked convincing.

It is no real criticism of Greenly's achievement in building the RH&DR to say that he made mistakes in engineering. He broke so much new ground that it would have been very surprising if every detail came right first time. But on returning to New Romney in the Spring of 1929, Howey set to work with a will to change everything Greenly had done which displeased him, a process which took several years. One of the first changes, carried out that autumn, was to realign and straighten the tracks through New Romney station. Serpentine to start with, these had been made positively zig-zag by the awkward way in which the Dungeness extension had been squeezed through the site. Howey swept away

Greenly's carefully laid out blind curves on the approach, demolished the two carriage sheds and the carpenter's shop, and laid over a quarter of a mile of rerouted main line, on which one slight curve replaced four sharp ones.

But perhaps the worst early technical problem was the fact that the 4–8–2s tended to derail on points. They had a fairly long rigid wheelbase, and Greenly had not allowed very much sideplay on the leading bogie. The standard and very nicely-made Theakston turnouts with a 1 in 8 crossing and 7ft switches were just a shade too sharply curved to suit them. This was a fairly serious embarrassment, and it resulted in both locomotives being more or less withdrawn, as rectification would have been a difficult matter. Colonel Theakston hastily produced a new set of standard turnouts with a 1 in 10 crossing and 9ft switches, and these were laid in to replace most of the earlier ones. But after 1927 *Hercules* saw only limited use, while *Samson* was laid aside completely and quarried for spare parts; by 1939 it was a rusting and derelict hulk.

Two other design problems manifested themselves with the locomotives. One was that they rode in far too lively a manner. Greenly had fitted them with coil springs throughout, following model rather than main line practice. But coil springs, though they flex freely, tend to bounce, lacking the shock-absorbing effect of friction between the leaves of a laminated spring. Even the radial trailing wheels of all the locomotives had coil springs, placed inside dummy leaf springs which were carried outside the frames for the sake of a correct appearance, an amazing piece of misplaced ingenuity. Arthur Binfield, Jackson, Rigby's boy apprentice, was induced to volunteer to ride on a flat truck pushed ahead of *Hercules* at speed, leaning out to check whether the engine's wheels ever actually lifted off the rails. He found that they did, but lived to tell the tale. One by one the 4–6–2s returned to Paxmans for alteration, having leaf springs fitted throughout except on the leading bogies, where room could not be found for them. The 4–8–2s were left unaltered, except for the radial wheels. The other modification was the removal of Greenly's singularly ineffective grid-type smokebox superheaters. Plenty of main line experiments before 1914 had proved that unless the locomotive was working exceptionally hard, grids of this pattern did nothing whatever to raise steam temperatures but more often seemed to operate as steam coolers. Greenly nevertheless believed in them, as did Martens, but at New Romney they gradually disappeared after his

No 9 *Doctor Syn*, as delivered to New Romney in 1931, complete with Vanderbilt tender fitted with vacuum-operated scoop for the watertroughs Howey intended to install at Greatstone. The amazing array of oilboxes and mechanical lubricators on the running plate was thinned out later. (*J. T. Holder*)

departure and were not mourned.

Problems with the early coaches have already been mentioned, and were less easy to put right. In 1930 Theakston drew Howey's attention to the Gibbins patent spring-frame bogie, an unusual design being promoted at that time by the Gloucester Railway Carriage & Wagon Company. As its name implies, this is a very simple design of bogie in which the axleboxes are held top and bottom by a pair of laminated springs each as long as the bogie wheelbase. All the expensive machined parts, horns and links and slides, were thus abolished and the frame reduced to a mere bracket to which springs, bolsters, and brake gear were bolted. No cheaper bogie could possibly be imagined. It did suffer

Howey standing beside the Theakston-Ford locomotive at New Romney in 1930. Neither fast nor beautiful, this short-lived machine was the first used in the attempt to run the winter services economically. (*J. T. Holder*)

from the defect that a broken spring would cause the whole structure to fall apart, though some stops on the frame were intended to catch the axles and avoid a derailment if this happened, and for this reason the design never found favour on any main line. But for the RH&DR it offered good prospects, and Howey decided to try it. At the same time he had been attracted by the ease and economy of maintenance of roller bearings, which needed greasing once a year, compared with the solid conventional bearings on the original coaches, which needed oiling after every trip round the railway.

The eight Clayton coaches were the first to be fitted with roller-bearing Gibbins bogies in 1930, and their riding greatly improved, while the rollers were completely successful. Howey then decided to fit similar bogies to the ex-Eskdale ballast hoppers and to try the effect of articulating the four-wheeled coaches using Gibbins bogies between the units, the outer ends of the resulting five- and nine-car sets being left riding on single axles. The improvement here was less marked, and in any case these coach bodies were rather spartan and unappealing. The articulation programme was therefore stopped before very many vehicles had been converted.

Much faster and rather better-looking than its predecessor; the modified Silver Ghost Rolls-Royce, with its first body, at New Romney. This machine could pull light trains at 60mph, and worked the winter services through the 1930s. (*P. B. Fincken*)

In 1934 Howey decided on radical action. All the four-wheelers would be scrapped, and replaced by new bogie coaches on 16ft steel frames by Hudson of Leeds; some would have Gibbins bogies salvaged from the articulated sets, others new bogies of Hudson's standard design, though again fitted with roller bearings. The new bodies were built locally, by the Hythe Cabinet Works, and were very lavish and comfortable. Each vehicle seated only eight, the same as a four-wheeler, but in a completely enclosed saloon with four doors, soft upholstered seats, and lots of leg-room. They were considerably more comfortable than most main line third-class stock of the day. The bodywork was much more in the style of a motorcar than an ordinary carriage, with car-type door handles and catches, and wind-down windows, while the actual body structure was of sheet steel and aluminium on a light wooden frame. By June 1936 no fewer than 54 of these bogie coaches, plus two matching vans, had been built, and all the unaltered four-wheelers and most of the articulated sets had been scrapped or sold. Some of the Gibbins bogies from the latter were used under tenders, all of which had originally been fitted with Greenly's bogies, and so drivers also benefited from the improved riding. They also benefited from rather more predictable brakes, since now about two-thirds of the coaches had vacuum equipment, transferred from the scrapped four-wheelers.

Both the other changes to Greenly's original work were at New Romney station. All three tracks in the original locomotive shed had been approached over a turntable, and one morning in

September 1935 the inevitable happened; *Northern Chief* fell into the turntable pit and boxed in all the other engines. Howey sped off to Barnstaple, where the equipment of the just-closed 2ft gauge Lynton & Barnstaple line was being auctioned, and purchased the turntable from Pilton Yard. This was laid in clear of the shed entrance and the old turntable taken out and eventually scrapped. At least that kind of incident could not happen again.

Howey had never been much interested in workshops and having had such difficulty at New Romney had decided by 1930 to do as little construction and repair work as possible on the railway, depending on outside contractors instead. The machine shop was therefore closed down after Chaldecott left, and for a while locomotives were sent back each year to Paxmans for overhaul and even for such inconsiderable tasks as preparing for boiler inspections. By 1935 the enormous expense of doing things this way had become obvious, particularly since all the engines were still quite new and very little heavy work needed doing to them. On cost grounds, therefore, Howey changed his mind again and decided to have light and medium work done at New Romney. The old machine shop was not reopened, except for the wheel lathe, a nineteenth-century relic which Chaldecott had left behind (and which is still in service); instead, a small erecting shop, fitted with a pair of gantry cranes in the roof capable of lifting a locomotive off its wheels, was built nearby.

The run-down of manufacturing capacity at New Romney left Howey with a problem over the two new locomotives. He now had various parts for them including boilers, wheels, and cylinders, but no design as to how they should be assembled. Various locomotive building firms were approached to see whether they would be

One of the 4–8–2s, probably *Hercules*, on a Dungeness–Hythe train at the short-lived platform adjacent to the SR station at New Romney, confusingly signboarded Littlestone-on-Sea, about 1928. (*Henry Greenly*)

prepared to help, and ultimately the Yorkshire Engine Co in Sheffield agreed to finish the job. After a year in store, the parts were shipped off to their works and the engines were completed, still without any proper drawings, which do not exist to this day. On the whole Yorkshire Engine did a very good job, presumably from sketches on the backs of used envelopes, though the two machines have always differed in many details. They were given Vanderbilt tenders which were fitted with vacuum-operated water scoops, the only concrete evidence of Howey's one-time scheme to lay down water troughs near Greatstone. When finally delivered to the railway in 1931, they became No 9 *Doctor Syn* and No 10 *Black Prince*. They have always lacked headlights, which spoils their Canadian resemblance, but they soon had real American five-tone chime whistles, from Crosby of Boston, the first of their kind in Britain. Gresley in due course heard and admired them, as Howey had in Canada, and later on acquired some more for the LNER *Cock o' the North* 2–8–2s and the A4 streamlined Pacifics.

Nos 9 and 10 did not see much service on winter trains. Howey may have been impressed first by the discomfort suffered on the footplate of one of the earlier engines in winter storms, but he was impressed second by the very limited amount of traffic offering for a daily service in winter and the amount of money he was losing by running one. This at least could be reduced by having an internal-combustion locomotive of some kind. In 1929 therefore Colonel Theakston supplied one. It was a very curious machine indeed, not resembling anything on any other railway in Britain (except a near twin at Ravenglass) but having something in common perhaps with the famous *Galloping Goose* railcars introduced around the same time on the Rio Grande Southern Railroad in Colorado. A Model T Ford engine and gearbox was mounted on a frame, supported at one end by an ordinary Gibbins bogie and at the other by a rigidly-mounted double pair of wheels, the first axle consisting of the original Model T differential, the second coupled by chain to it. Possibly it could have been described as a 4–4–0, or (if the differential had not been locked up) even more accurately as a 4–1–3; viewed as a power unit, it was essentially a motor car with eight wheels and no steering, and unable to move at more than a crawl in reverse. It could not do much more than a crawl going forward either, being geared for a maximum of about 15mph, which limited Howey's enthusiasm for it. It was provided with a wooden steeple-cab body, reminiscent of certain early electric locomotives.

However unglamorous and unreliable it was, the Theakston-Ford certainly pointed the way how to deal with the winter trains, which were rarely steam-worked thereafter. In autumn 1930 Howey decided to build another, better, locomotive on the same general principles, and to this end sacrificed the Rolls-Royce Silver Ghost shooting brake which he had purchased in 1914. The resulting locomotive was of course much more powerful and also faster; very considerably faster, in fact, and perfectly capable of reaching

When the inconvenient platform next to the SR station at New Romney was abandoned, Dungeness to Hythe trains had to stop in the main station in such a way that passengers had to stand on the down main line to board or alight. Here a school party looking for seats on a long and crowded train stands clear while the two locomotives cut off and go for water. (*Fox Photos*)

speeds of a mile a minute. He was once timed at 60.2mph with it, hauling four Clayton coaches. The original Silver Ghost engine did not long survive, breaking a connecting rod at speed with dramatic results, but was replaced by another. The Rolls locomotive in its original form was a very practical machine, with a good cab, powerful headlights and cowcatcher, and fitted with vacuum brake equipment; after 1931 it ran the winter service regularly until the outbreak of the second world war. Its main foible was that since the vacuum exhauster was driven off the crankshaft, the train brakes would come on if the engine revs fells below a certain speed; this meant that to slow down but not stop for level crossings one had to coast in neutral with a foot on the accelerator. The Theakston-Ford was broken up in the mid-1930s; the Rolls received a new motorcar type body in 1946 and survived until 1961. The Rolls-Royce Company was traditionally very snooty about people who made unauthorised modifications to their cars; L. T. C. Rolt in *Landscape with Machines* records how they refused on one occasion to supply him with spare parts for a particular customer's car which their records showed had been fitted with another firm's front-wheel brakes until these had been removed. Howey's insolence in converting one of their products into a locomotive, narrow-gauge at that, on which he had taken great care to make the famous radiator as conspicuous as possible, was so outrageous that the company decided instead to ride with the punch, and the machine was described with approval in the *Rolls-Royce Bulletin* for July 1933.

But the Rolls was not the fastest thing on wheels. There was yet a third device, something of a motor roller skate, which Howey had built in 1929. It seated only one person in comfort, and was powered by a JAP 6hp motor cycle engine, driving one pair of wheels direct through a rubber belt without clutch or gearbox. To start it, you pushed it along and when it fired you jumped aboard before it left you behind. Howey used this deadly weapon as his own personal transport up

The War Department's Austin-engined 'light locomotive', built for duty on the branch to the Mirror, as running in RH&DR service in 1947. The driver is Jack Hook, who worked for the railway from 1926 to 1962, latterly as Foreman Platelayer. (*J. C. Flemons*)

and down the railway, and early one morning in the 1930s reached Hythe from New Romney in 'even time' – $8\frac{1}{4}$ miles in $8\frac{1}{4}$ minutes! This must have involved sustained speeds of at least 70mph, with no slowing down for any of the five level crossings; certainly it was a form of Russian Roulette. It may be doubted whether anybody to this day has ever equalled this time along the main coast road, which has considerably more and worse curves than the railway.

With all these additional locomotives there was, by 1931, no place left for *The Bug*. It had done good work in the construction period, but Greenly's extravagant ideas of operating with shunting engines had been dropped, and since its maximum speed was about the same as the Theakston-Ford, Howey found little attraction in it. After several years lying at the back of the shed alongside *Samson*, during which time both machines were nearly sold on several occasions, once to a concern in Ceylon, in November 1933 *The Bug* was finally sold for £150 to a Mr Kamiya of Blackpool, who had a firm regrettably called 'Honeymoon Express Ltd'. For a further £270 he bought six four-wheeled coaches plus bogies to articulate them. A little later the outfit was resold to Belfast Zoo, where it operated on a small circular line with hairpin bends until 1939. Mr Kamiya offered £800 for *Samson*, but Howey thought this was not enough.

By 1938 all these processes of change and development had been completed, and the railway was ready to settle down like any normal commercial enterprise and try to earn a living. It is instructive to consider the financial position it had reached. After some very large losses in the first four seasons, due mainly to over-lavish working and staffing, and to running a steam-worked service throughout the winter with all the stations manned, after 1931 it began to turn the corner and showed some modest profits. These were due partly to radical economies urged on Howey by the Holders, such as running the winter trains with the Rolls-Royce and a conductor-guard on the train to sell tickets; other cuts like dispensing with the three full-time gardeners, raising the level of the track through the tunnel at New Romney to avoid having to pump it dry continually (this involved lowering the roofs of all the older coaches), and allowing the right-of-way to become rank with weeds. There were some positive changes as well, such as the use of better coaches. From 1935 to 1937 the accounts again showed losses, but these were due to the fact that under the Railway Accounts Acts the new coaches, since they replaced older ones, had to be charged in full against that year's revenue, and on any ordinary reckoning these years would have been profitable. Robert Hardie, in charge of day-to-day management, had obviously got a good grip of the operation, and things rather went to pieces after he died, particularly as J. Jackson, his second-in-command, resigned rather than take over Hardie's responsibilities at a lower salary than Hardie had received. Not for the first time, Howey lost out by not treating his senior staff with any generosity. 1938 was a poor year and would have shown a deficit on any basis; by its end, the books showed an accumulated deficit on Revenue Account of £13,318.

This of course was money Howey had to find, over and above the actual cost of building the railway as shown on Capital Account. It is interesting to summarise this and compare it with Henry Greenly's 1926 estimates. Of course, this is not quite fair; Greenly was estimating for $8\frac{1}{4}$ miles of single line with four locomotives, and Howey had achieved $13\frac{1}{2}$ miles of double line with nine locomotives, plus all the other extras mentioned. All the same, the money had been spent and had to come from somewhere.

	Actual net cost to 31.12.38 £	Greenly estimate 1926 £
Land and Buildings	20,745	3,255
Permanent Way and Works	52,146	15,482
Housing	13,443	—
Plant and Equipment	4,277	882
Locomotives and Rolling Stock	39,982	5,700
	130,593	25,319
Add:		
Deficit on Revenue Account	13,318	—
Preliminary Expenses	—	800
Total Outlay	£143,911	£26,119

Greenly had not been too far out on Permanent Way and Works, considering that about three times as much track had been laid as he contemplated; and some of the excess in Building and in Plant was of course due to the RH&DR having to establish its own workshops after all. Detailed records show that Howey had to pay well over the valuation for land, for the sake of peace and quiet, and that Greenly was way out over locomotives and particularly coaches. Housing was another item not originally budgeted for. It included not only Howey's and Hardie's

The start of work on the aeroplane detection experiments, about 1929; the WD 15in gauge line to Maddieson's Camp, with RH&DR Heywood-type wagons in the foreground. (*H. S. Francis*)

Howey's daughter Gloria on *Green Goddess* about 1938, watched over by her regular driver, an ex-Great Eastern man. In the background, one of the Eskdale 6ton ballast waggons. (*Fox Photos*)

bungalows (Greenly's had been sold in 1931) but also 12 terrace houses in Station Road, New Romney, still called Melbourne Villas, intended for staff. These had been mortgaged to raise £6,000, and other shareholders had subscribed for a total of 1,802 shares, but Howey had had to find the rest of the money, totalling some £136,000, himself. This was the equivalent of something over £3 million in 1980. One of Howey's favourite stories was about the coach driver in the late 1930s who told his awed passengers as they got back on board after a ride

This dog-eared builders' photograph of Canadian Pacific heavy 4–6–2 No 2300 is the one which was pinned to A. L. S. Richardson's drawing board as he worked on the designs for RH&DR Nos 9 and 10. The Yorkshire Engine Company may also have used it; but the eventual resemblance of the finished locomotives to their prototype was, for the reasons explained in the text, much less close than for the Gresley-type 4–6–2s.

on the RH&DR, '10 years ago the man who owns this railway just had two locomotives, and now he's a millionaire'.

One technical embarrassment resulted from the fact that the railway company had spent much more than it was legally entitled to. The second Light Railway Order increased its share capital to £51,000 and borrowing powers to £17,000, at which figures they remained until 1974. This meant that it was entitled to raise and borrow only a total of £68,000. To regularise the position, Howey made the company a gift of £61,680 in June 1932; this was simply a paper transaction which had the effect of writing down the value of the assets in the company's books to a figure generally around half their actual cost.

Even if Howey never saw any financial return on this investment, it clearly gave him a great deal of enjoyment. All the memories of the RH&DR in the 1930s make it clear that everybody got a lot of sheer fun out of it, Howey included. Then as now, it attracted a nucleus of staff who quite simply enjoyed the work enough to accept the fairly low pay. The number of permanent employees had to be reduced after 1931, and even with the traditional flexibility of working in a small company the peak train service could only be run with the aid of a band of cheerful volunteer conscripts known rather ambiguously as the 'slave drivers'. These tended to be railway-minded students and young men, friends of Howey's son, or the Holders, or of Colonel R. B. Tyrrell, a

miniature railway enthusiast who had purchased Greenly's bungalow, and his son R. M. Tyrrell, always called Sam; Terry Holder's cousin Nigel, another fast-car-fancier; Dan Crittall of Crittall Windows; Sir John Samuel, who later had a very fine 7¼in gauge railway of his own, the Greywood Central, purchased after his untimely death by Ian Allan and re-established as the Great Cockrow; and Howey's nephew and co-pilot on Monte Carlo rallies, Andrew Bowring.

During the summer holidays these youngsters would be shedded in a dormitory-hovel behind the signalbox at New Romney, and woken up each morning by a maid bringing a tray of cups of tea across from *Red Tiles*. All day they were in charge of a locomotive, and woe betide anybody whose mastery of the machine or whose behaviour was in any way less than totally up to professional main line standards. Sam Tyrrell later wrote:

After a week's instruction on the footplate with regular drivers I was considered competent to drive and soon became versed in Captain Howey's Seven Commandments for the Loco Department. They were:
thou shalt not emit dark smoke;
thou shalt not blow off steam while standing;
thous shalt not fire up in stations;
thou shalt not use the blower except when absolutely essential;
thou shalt take on a goodly proportion of slack when coaling up;
when thou hast five spare minutes thou shalt employ them in cleaning thy locomotive;
thou shalt not run over any sheep.

Howey was apt to show up unpredictably along the line, and carried a telescope in his SSK Mercedes for unobserved observations, so there was no room for any slacking. But if it was hard work it was very satisfying, and one economy had not been made; the railway still employed a firedropper/tubecleaner, who took over the engine at the end of the day and saved the driver the chore of putting it away. On the other hand, if a driver reported a low joint somewhere along the line, Howey would often press-gang a party to go out the same evening and put it right, often including the butler Biggs and the chauffeur Webb. One particular occupant of the tubecleaner's position at this period, a character whom Tony Howey christened 'The Golden Centipede', lent a flavour of his own to the operation; he believed in maximum economy of effort, and having a dirty job to do every day saw no point in taking a bath until the end of the season.

Life at *Red Tiles* was very light-hearted. Often enough during the summer there were tremendous parties, largely for the young railwaymen's benefit; Folkestone was then a rather livelier place than it has been in recent years and carloads of actresses would be brought along from the Leas Theatre, or the Hippodrome at Dover, as well as any other eligible young females. Something of all this cheerfulness obviously communicated itself to the customers, and the RH&DR soon became something of a national institution. It was perhaps immortalised for the first time by Alfred Hitchcock, in his version of *The Lady Vanishes*, filmed in 1937. When Michael Redgrave, the young hero, climbed aboard the footplate of the express in order to drive across the frontier to safety, the villains having shot the driver and fireman, Naunton Wayne said to him 'I say, you don't know how to make this go, do you?', getting the answer 'Of course I do, I once drove an engine on the Dymchurch line'.

Things were brightened even further on occasion when Howey played host to some of his Brooklands friends, many of whom shared his railway interest. After all, Gresley's Pacifics were also able to run at three-figure speeds, otherwise only reached by racing motorists, so a healthy respect for steam engineering and its achievements was only natural. Perhaps the most dreadful escapade, long kept a frightful secret lest they hear of it at the Ministry, occurred when Henry Segrave paid a visit to New Romney. Segrave was certainly the greatest British racing driver of the 1920s, and twice holder of the Land Speed Record (203mph in 1927, 231mph in 1929). Howey challenged him to a locomotive race; the timetable was cancelled, the railway cleared, and both men set off side by side for Hythe, running on parallel tracks, Howey on

Hurricane and Segrave on *Typhoon*. Apparently it was neck and neck. There were also a number of professional railwaymen as frequent and honoured guests; apart from Gresley, these included Bill Sparshatt, the speed demon driver of the East Coast Main Line during the 1930s.

Howey did not forsake motor racing entirely; he remained keenly interested in cars and twice drove his Mercedes in the Monte Carlo Rally. He maintained a small stable of impressive motors at New Romney, including for a time the first of Zborowski's famous *Chitty Bang Bangs*, which had been left to him. He was always an impressively good driver on public roads, extremely fast, but with sure judgment and anticipation so that it was a pleasure to ride with him, even for nervous passengers. But he took no further part in set-piece motor racing following the death of his brother in August 1926, three weeks after the Duke of York's visit to New Romney. Richard Howey had been taking part in a three-day event on public roads at Boulogne, where eyebrows were raised at the risks even before the first accident. In a hill-climb trial at Baincthun he skidded off the road in his Ballot, struck a tree, and was killed instantly. J. E. P. Howey and his wife were summoned by telegram from New Romney, but there was little they could do. Returning that same evening to England with the wreck, they arranged for the ferry to heave-to in mid-Channel and the car was quietly pushed overboard.

Howey's son Tony was a reluctant conscript. Aged 15 when the RH&DR opened, he probably had too much of his father's toy too soon, and never did any driving; in fact it is not too much to say he positively detested the railway. He was a cheerful young man, however, who if set to clipping tickets would clip a lot of other things as well and enliven the platform with loud cries like 'change here for Cosham, Cookham, and Nosham' and similar irreverences. His father did a lot of driving himself, which occasionally led to odd incidents. He always liked to tell the story about how at Hythe on a hot day he was on the engine tieless and coatless, but wearing Old Etonian braces. It is always one of the charming things about Etonians that they choose such arcane means of identifying themselves, conjuring up curious speculations about the nature of the occasions for braces-display, but all the same this was one of them. It so happened that another OE was taking his family for a ride on the train and came up to inspect the engine. Seeing the driver's braces, he looked appalled and quickly pulled a

The original short train-shed at Hythe was soon doubled in length, to accommodate half the length of an average train. In this 1947 view, *Green Goddess* is uncoupled from an arriving train to draw forward into the release road, as the passengers stream past. (*A. C. K. Ware*)

pound note out of his wallet. Pressing it into the speechless Howey's hand, he muttered 'sorry to see you've come down to this, old man', and hastily disappeared.

During the early 1930s the Army began to experiment with acoustic detectors. This proved to be one of technology's blind alleys, and John Masters describes how it later became a classic example of how not to organise scientific research. 'In the 1930s both the army and the air force were concerned with the problem of detecting enemy aircraft at a greater distance than the existing searchlights and sound rangers could do. Each service gave the scientific establishment an object to be achieved. The army said they wanted searchlights and sound rangers that could pick up an aircraft at 30,000ft and 20 miles instead of the then limit of 20,00ft and 10 miles. In due course they got what they had asked for − better searchlights, better sound rangers. The air force defined their object more accurately: to detect and track aircraft from as great a distance as possible. They got radar.'

Most of the army's experimental work was carried out near the RH&DR, with one group of sound mirrors on the hills above Hythe and another near Maddieson's Camp. The latter included some large reinforced concrete structures of curious shape, whose construction would require tons of materials and many workmen; since there was no road access, the

RH&DR was asked to put in a branch line about ½-mile long to the site, completed about 1933. Materials were duly brought in by rail, and until work finished about 1937 there was also a daily workmen's train from New Romney and sometimes Hythe, usually worked by a light petrol locomotive belonging to the War Department. During the winter one track was made available all the time to the army, and the RH&DR service operated on the other. Howey noticed that the new line served an area where shingle could be excavated for sale as ballast, and began to build up a small trade in this; in 1933 a steeply-graded track was put in climbing a ramp at one corner of Hythe station yard, to serve some hoppers where the stone could be transferred to road vehicles.

The WD branch line played a part in another matter. Following the opening of the Dungeness extension, housing development began all along the strip of coast between Greatstone and The Pilot, and in 1935 the Southern Railway proposed to divert its New Romney branch to run close to and parallel with the RH&DR to serve this new source of traffic. This diversion involved building nearly four miles of new line, increasing the length of the branch by two miles, but Sir Herbert Walker was still in command of the SR and it was still expansion-minded. Howey viewed this plan with a slightly jaundiced eye. He could hardly object to it on the grounds of diversion of his own traffic, but he had a different grievance. Ever since the RH&DR had opened, large numbers of main-line railwaymen on holiday had turned up expecting to be sold quarter-rate privilege tickets, which were available by agreement between all the railway companies existing in 1923 for all their staff freely over each others' lines. Howey honoured this understanding so far as visitors to his own railway were concerned, but got nothing for his own staff in return, except on the London & North Eastern; Gresley had pulled strings there. The other three companies had refused several times to do the same. At last Providence had given Howey a stick with which he could legitimately beat at least one of them. The SR's new line would have to cross over the RH&DR branch, and the SR confidently expected to do so on the level. Howey refused, and got the War Department to back him. A level crossing would be prejudicial to the defence of the realm. The RH&DR was there first; the SR would have to build a bridge and go over the top. There was still no movement on the privilege ticket issue, however, and the impasse remained until after the second world war, when finally a season's collection of PT Orders honoured by the RH&DR was placed without comment on the desk of the SR General Manager. He then had little option but to give in, and so honour was eventually satisfied.

5
The War

The summer holidays of 1939 were overshadowed by an increasingly alarming international situation and were cut short abruptly by the German invasion of Poland and the British declaration of war against Germany on Sunday 3 September. RH&DR services were curtailed at once to the basic daily winter schedule, but continued to operate. It was a confused period, with men being called to service in the forces and a great expansion of army camps and depots, and it all took time to organise. At first there was little happening on Romney Marsh, except the takeover on the first day of the war of the Boys' Camp property at St Mary's Bay, used first as a mobilisation centre. Howey contacted the camp at once and offered the railway's help with troop movements, and was taken at his word. The first troop trains ran on 5 September, shuttling from Hythe to St Mary's Bay, and consisting of 30 coaches with two engines at one end and three at the other (in later years heavier trains were run with fewer machines!). Writing about this years later, Lt-Col P. G. R. Burford of the Artists' Rifles mentions that the battalion's railway warrant could be extended from Sandling Junction, where they detrained, to St Mary's Bay – 'how it was done, I was never sure, but it was'. Knowing the military bureaucracy it seems a fair bet that it wasn't, and that Howey knew it wouldn't be. Not that it mattered.

Gradually the area was taken over entirely for military purposes, and as the Germans swept across northern France in May and June 1940 the wide-open beaches between Hythe and Rye became once again the first line of the defence of England. The RH&DR had ceased working before April, and all staff except a couple of caretakers discharged. During June and July, most of the civilian population living in the area was evacuated, and it became clear that if the threatened German invasion were to take place, it would almost certainly involve landings on these beaches. After 1945 the captured documents detailing the plans for Hitler's Operation Sea Lion proved that this was indeed so, although the first landings would have been between Dungeness and Rye.

A new crop of defence works were hastily built, and there was a mushroom growth of bunkers and gun emplacements closely spaced near the beach, and at strategic points inland; many remain. The beaches were hastily blocked with barbed wire entanglements and thickets of tubular scaffolding, which had been found to jam up tank tracks nicely; some traces of these can also still be seen in certain tide conditions. The Somerset Light Infantry, having set out on what they thought was a journey to France, found themselves at the time of Dunkirk responsible for building these works in the section served by the RH&DR. Colonel (then Major) D. I. L. Beath, second-in-command of the Battalion, was a keen railway enthusiast, as was the adjutant, and they both leapt on the railway with cries of joy. Beath put forward the idea that not only would it be useful for military transport, but an armoured train could patrol it. A quick check revealed that the Battalion included a number of railwaymen, who were formed into a Railway Section. Thereupon the SLI took over the line outright,

For understandable reasons, photography was forbidden in the invasion area during the war, but an exception was made for the armoured train, though the censors did not release these official pictures for several years. Here it is at Dymchurch in autumn 1940. (*Imperial War Museum*)

with the minimum of reference to the War Office, of which perhaps as Territorials they were not in any case sufficiently respectful. Paperwork was set in motion to requisition it in proper legal form, but from June 1940 onwards it was an army railway in fact. *Hercules* and two of the ex-Eskdale bogie ballast wagons were rushed off to the nearby Southern Railway works at Ashford, and returned soon afterwards armoured and fitted with two Lewis Guns (one on an anti-aircraft mounting) and a Boyes Anti-Tank Rifle on each wagon – not very fearsome weapons, except perhaps in the second case to the user, but the best available. A Bofors gun later replaced the Boyes. The armour was also fairly minimal, consisting of steel plates protecting boiler and smokebox only on the engine, and steel sidesheets protecting the men in the centre well on each wagon, which still remained open to the sky. However, the train would be a fairly difficult target to hit, and the armour provided adequately against bullets and splinters. A direct hit by bomb or shell would have knocked it over anyhow.

Until the danger disappeared, by autumn 1941, the armoured train remained with steam up at all times, based mainly in a special siding near Dymchurch under an artificial hill built of camouflage nets and scrim. The Battalion HQ was at Dymchurch station, which was reinforced with blast walls consisting of foot-thick concrete laced with old tram rails to give some protection against air attack; air raid shelters were also built in the yard at New Romney.

The Somersets did not remain in charge of the railway for very long, and various units, including one Canadian, had it successively. Some outfits had a sufficient sprinkling of professional railwaymen who knew how things worked, others did not. The Canadians, for example, were foxed by British-type signalboxes and frustrated by the need to pull certain levers before others; they solved that difficulty by smashing the interlocking with a sledgehammer. Some quite spectacular misadventures were only narrowly averted. Beath himself drove the first train of the army regime to Hythe during the Battle of Britain, which provided a noisy background plus occasional showers of spent bullets from overhead. He was in trouble for steam, and finally ebbed to a halt with the engine standing on the girders of the New Cut Bridge. Here he set to busily making up his fire, clearing out and dumping red-hot clinker and ashes; after 20 minutes of hard work he was able to proceed. All the time he had been conscious of another rather scruffy group of soldiers some distance away by the canal bank, an apparently ill-disciplined lot who kept on shouting and waving their arms about in a most unmilitary manner. It seemed better to pay them no attention. Later on he found out that they had just mined the bridge so that it could be blown up if the Germans landed, and he had been cleaning his fire out onto their demolition charges.

Meanwhile the paperwork about requisitioning the railway was making its stately way through proper channels to the War Office, where in December it finally reached the desk in the Home Railways Department of Major (later Colonel) Kenneth Cantlie. Cantlie felt that this was the ultimate proof of how everybody had gone mad that summer. What possible use could the RH&DR be to the defence of Britain? Did whoever had started this absurd hare even know it was only 15in gauge? With a few crisp sentences he flatly rejected the idea and sent the file bouncing back to the Division. Immediately afterwards, with one of those nice strokes of poetic justice that so seldom actually happen in real life, he was made Director of Military Railways in the invasion area, and arrived on Romney Marsh in time to receive his own letter. But having sized up the situation he knew he would have to insist on the requisitioning going through, and it was eventually backdated to 15 June 1940.

By the time Cantlie arrived the railway was in a bad way. Apart from the effects of untutored operators, the Luftwaffe had begun to pay it a great deal of attention, and continued to do so during 1941 and 1942. Possibly the fact that it was the first railway that a bomber approaching across the Channel would see might have had something to do with it; as a double track, it could also be readily mistaken for a standard gauge main line from the air. Many bombs had already been dropped on it, particularly around New Romney; a near miss on the engine shed had lifted one locomotive off the elevated rails and dropped

The armoured train, *Hercules* in the centre, passing some hastily-repaired bomb damage on the line near Dymchurch. (*Imperial War Museum*)

it down awkwardly across them, where rerailing it was a tiresome job. Another had been a direct hit on a shelter in the yard, killing six men inside it. Quite a number of coaches had also been badly damaged.

During the late 1920s and early 1930s Cantlie, a Crewe-trained engineer by profession, had been eight years in China, then suffering much devastation from civil war, and had probably as much experience as any man in Britain in getting shattered railways running again quickly. On his first visit to New Romney he stood on the footbridge and looked around at the bombed shops and carriages all over the yard, and Brigadier Blakey who was with him said 'Well, Cantlie, you must think yourself back in China during the civil wars.' Cantlie had been thinking exactly that. The first thing to do was to put the right men in charge. He made the Royal Engineers at last responsible for running the line, and installed a team of 15 men under CQMS Blower. Things looked up rapidly.

The repairable engines and coaches were repaired, the workshops re-established, the stores sorted out and added to with help from the Southern Railway, and a routine was set going for the next couple of years. The army soon discovered that most of the vacuum brake equipment on the coaches was inoperable through neglect, and that was put right as well. Trains were run as required during the week, for troop movements and bringing in supplies, and at the weekends five engines worked a recreational service for off-duty soldiers, bringing them in to civilisation at Hythe. This was very popular with the men, but caused terrible trouble with HQ at

the end of the year because it was found that receipts had exceeded expenditure by £50, and King's Regulations did not allow any army activity to make a profit. A certain amount of military method was also brought in. For example, the Sappers were appalled to find that none of the coaches or wagons had ever been numbered, and instituted a numbering system at once. This enabled a proper mileage-based maintenance routine to be set up for the first time.

One interesting further sidelight on prewar methods was shown when for the first time an army train ran over a sheep. Cantlie was presented with a claim by the farmer concerned, strangely enough for a pedigree ewe in lamb. It transpired that Howey had always paid up, on the nail, any sum demanded. Now that the line had been requisitioned these cash transactions were impossible, and Cantlie passed the claim up through Group to QMG(Claims) War Office, thinking that the farmer was likely to find a tougher adversary than the kind-hearted Captain. He did. There were few other claims, and the farmers began to repair the fences themselves.

Passenger services still operated the whole length of the line, although the Dungeness area was walled off behind immense constructions of barbed wire and scaffolding. The railway threaded its way inconspicuously through gaps in these where larger vehicles, including of course German ones, could not follow. It was intended that the armoured train should operate here if a landing ever took place. For a while Cantlie was tempted to extend the RH&DR from Dungeness to Camber Sands, linking up with the three-foot gauge railway from Rye, also in use by the army. This would have filled the gap in the defence line, but as the likelihood of invasion dwindled the case for this project weakened and ultimately nothing was done.

During the late summer and autumn of 1940 the skies over the whole of South-East England were by day the scene of fighter battles, and nowhere more than near the coast, where they continued only somewhat less fiercely during 1941. One rather macabre feature unique to Romney Marsh was the number of aeroplanes, of both sides, which simply flew into the ground and disappeared. A fighter shot down, possibly in a vertical power dive, would hit the soft soil at something approaching the speed of sound and be swallowed up with so little trace on the surface that unless the spot was marked at once it became impossible to find. With powerful metal detectors

the wreck, still complete, could have been found 20ft or 30ft down, and during the 1970s a considerable number were dug up in this way for museums. But nobody had time to do that sort of thing in 1940 and so the area was an unprofitable one for the scrap metal scavenging units which collected and recycled aerial debris in other parts of the country. The crew of the RH&DR armoured train were in several incidents, and claimed to have shot down a Dornier. The SR New Romney branch train also scored one against the Luftwaffe, when a low-flying Heinkel strafed the D3 class 0-4-4T near Greatstone and managed to shoot off its dome. But it was a Pyrrhic victory; an instant later the aircraft flew into the roaring column of steam escaping from the boiler and was blown out of control, hitting the ground a little distance away. Also based on the SR branch for a period was one of the gigantic rail-mounted 15in guns; these had to be used on a curve in order to be aimed laterally, and the great horseshoe bend at Lydd-on-Sea where the line swung through almost 180 degrees was an ideal location.

There was one other incident involving an RH&DR train, and it so happened that Cantlie was nearby when it occurred. Out in the middle of the Willop a low-flying German pilot saw engine No 9 steaming across his flight path and aimed a bomb at it; but he was too low for the bomb to behave properly. Landing at a very oblique angle, it slithered on its side across the field, struck the track a few yards ahead of the engine, but failed to explode until it had ricochetted into the air again. It then went off 100ft or so further away, forming a crater still visible 40 years later and blasting a great shower of mud and turf all over the place. In striking the rails it had buckled them, and this derailed the train. All the driver knew was that he had come off the road with a shattering explosion, to find himself covered in mud. Cantlie heard the bang and walked across to see what had happened. He found the driver shaking with nerves and about to get hysterical. Realising that something had to be done quickly to prevent him breaking down, he roasted him for having a dirty footplate. Instantly the driver forgot the war; with the familiar enemy of a nit-witted spit-and-polish damn-fool of an officer to contend with, he thought he knew where he was and got so angry he pulled himself together.

Not that there was much spit and polish about at the time. Howey spent the war living near Ascot, driving a YMCA canteen van for the benefit of soldiers in training on the surrounding heathlands. One day in 1941 when things had got a little quieter, he managed to obtain a permit to visit New Romney with Captain Holder, and they spent several happy hours in the shed cleaning up some of the engines. This got them into trouble; it was forcibly pointed out that gleaming brass and shining paint were very conspicuous from the air and would attract undesirable attention. Dirty engines were much preferred, and they had to grease over their handiwork.

After the invasion threat died away, Cantlie was posted elsewhere to deal with railways in other places, and there was something of a lull until by 1942 and 1943 work had swung round towards preparing for another invasion, going in the opposite direction. Two projects for this were under way near New Romney by late 1943. One, the construction on the beach at Littlestone of some of the great concrete pontoons for Mulberry harbours, did not concern the RH&DR; the other one did. The were to be several submarine pipelines to supply the Normandy beaches with petrol, consisting of miles of welded steel pipes unrolled onto the sea bed from giant floating drums, one of which was to run from Dungeness. The project was named PLUTO (Pipe Line Under The Ocean). Steel pipes arrived at New Romney on the SR and were transferred to 15in gauge wagons standing on rails laid between those of the standard gauge tranship siding. They were then welded into lengths of about 200yd on the RH&DR platforms; since the mains electricity supply was not robust enough to carry the massive current needed, a large diesel generator set was installed under the station roof. The welded lengths were at first loaded onto the RH&DR for shipment to Dungeness; to augment the four-wheelers 21 16ft bogie coaches were stripped of their bodies and used for this traffic, as was the last surviving five-coach articulated set. The pipes were used for eight parallel buried lines from a railhead at Lydd SR station to a series of pumping stations near the beach. To preserve secrecy against air reconnaissance by the Germans the pumps were put into existing seaside cottages, gutted for the purpose. They pumped the petrol across to France, give or take a number of leaks; smoking was forbidden for miles around. After a while the RH&DR ceased to be used to carry these pipes, which were instead dragged along the formation by tracked crawler vehicles, which wrecked much of the permanent way between New Romney and Dungeness.

This second spell of wartime activity came to an end in spring 1944, by which time the army had ceased to use the railway. The Hythe to New Romney section had been derequisitioned earlier, and effectively shut down during the spring of 1943. But the area remained a military zone until the war ended, and Howey was not able to return to New Romney nor was the railway released to him until July 1945. It was pretty badly damaged, and it was not feasible, with the lack of labour and materials, to attempt any reopening that year. A mile of track near New Romney was however temporarily regauged to 10¼in to allow a token operation to run that summer with a small 0–6–0T which Howey had acquired in 1938. One essential first step was to prepare and present a large claim for compensation for damage to the government; another was to assemble the reconstruction team.

6
Post-war Boom and Decline

During the middle of the war Howey had promised Terence Holder a job when peace returned, running the RH&DR full time; 'providing', he said, 'you make it pay'. As soon as he was demobilised in October 1945, Holder took up the offer, and moved with his wife into the station bungalow at Dymchurch. With effect from the start of November he was appointed Manager, at £500 a year plus £250 expenses, and set about performing his side of the bargain.

Apart from Howey's temporary length of 10¼in gauge track at New Romney, little had yet been done to restore or reopen the railway. One major problem was a great shortage of labour. The local inhabitants had returned, but for a while all efforts had to go into getting homes and houses and basic services working again. Demobilisation was proceeding fairly slowly and many of the men were still in the forces, often in the Far East. Holder however had the idea of arranging for gangs of German prisoners of war, who were not to be allowed to return home for another couple of years, to be lent to the railway, and much of the reconstruction work was done by them. Some was

Laurel and Hardy on the footplate of No 10 during their 1947 visit, at Hythe.

make pleasure trips for over six years; but foreign travel was still difficult and indeed going very far at home was not easy. Besides, the railway had received a lot of publicity during the war, and pictures of the armoured train in particular had appeared all over the world. The author, as an 11-year-old schoolboy in New Zealand, remembers being electrified by seeing its photograph in the *New Zealand Herald*, occupying half the back page, during 1943. But fundamentally, the fact that something so purely devoted to pleasure and entertainment as the RH&DR had returned so soon, symbolised an enormously welcome return to normal life, especially as so much else was still so austere and difficult.

Something had to be done to handle the crowds, and after the Easter holiday had given warning of what was to come, urgent steps were taken to get as many coaches as possible into service before the summer. The first thing was to put extremely simple bodies, mere toastracks consisting of floors and seats, onto the 16 or more bare bogie frames which were all that was left of the 21 Hythe saloons, plus the surviving articulated set, all knocked down to carry pipe. Packed sardine-solid, with knees interlocked, it was feasible to compress 16 adults into each of the former. A proportion of children theoretically allowed a bit more room, except that often two had to be packed into a single adult's space. For a while these very basic coaches ran without any roofs, and in fact it was not for several years that anybody travelling in one stood up just as it was about to go under a bridge. When the inevitable happened it was very fortunate that the victim recovered consciousness after a while and was ultimately none the worse for the experience. To prevent a recurrence, a light structure of angle iron and chicken wire was hastily screwed to each open coach, and this succeeded in keeping people's heads inside the loading gauge. It did not, however, answer the problem for long as one section of wire bulged out and scraped the soot off the roof of the tunnel under Littlestone Road one day, right on top of one hapless lady in a low-cut summer dress, who arrived at Greatstone looking like a member of the Black-and-White Minstrels, but not so happy. Chicken wire was then replaced by hardboard, after which these deplorable vehicles continued inexorably in service for years and years. It was not possible to withdraw the last three survivors until 1979.

The next step was to rebuild the ex-Eskdale ballast hoppers as passenger coaches. This was also done in a great hurry during 1947. One of the

also tackled by groups of local women, who had grown used during the war to pick and shovel work.

Between Hythe and New Romney the line was substantially intact, apart from some minor bomb damage. Hythe signalbox was still out of commission, but otherwise the track was in fair order. It was however very heavily overgrown and more or less impassable. Clearing this did not take many weeks, but more needed doing at New Romney. Most of the engines were in a reasonably serviceable state, although the engine shed floor had been filled several feet deep with ash and clinker. Coaches were obviously going to be a problem. Only 33 of the 54 Hythe saloons were still intact, plus the eight Claytons and one luggage van. There was no time to do more than smarten these up for service before the start of the 1946 season.

The railway was officially reopened between Hythe and New Romney on 1 March 1946 by the Mayors of the two towns. Holder had done his stuff to ensure publicity for the event, and at once, to Howey's complete astonishment, the trains were besieged by crowds of passengers. They were even larger than they had been during the opening season in 1927, and threatened to become a serious embarrassment. For most people, that spring was the first time it had been possible to

Hythe station about 1938. *Hercules* on a train of 1934 saloons; goods sidings on the right, with on the far right the ramp leading to the top of the ballast bins, next to the old manager's house.

six had disappeared during the war, according to rumour to form part of a road block, and two of the others had been incorporated into the armoured train. All five survivors were sent away to a firm in Ashford which stripped off the old steel sides and ends, and put on some remarkably flimsy timber and aluminium saloon bodies with seats running lengthways; these were quite soon replaced by some rather better 20-seat closed bodies with sliding doors. Unfortunately removing the sides left the frames rather weak, and over the years these vehicles slowly developed a noticeable sag in the middle. But with successive rebodyings they lasted quite well and were very effective platform-clearers; without their 100 extra seats the railway could hardly have coped with the continuing record traffic.

The final, and rather desperate, step taken to increase the number of coaches was to purchase the Eaton Railway lock stock and barrel from the Duke of Westminster in 1947. The last two steam engines at Eaton Hall had been cut up for scrap during the war, but three bogie coaches and a van, built around 1897, were acquired as well as various other items. These ancient wooden-framed vehicles were in fair order, having seen little use, though their bogies were not intended to run at Romney speeds and Heywood's original rubber block suspension had perished, so they rode extremely badly. However they had to be pressed into service at once, though after a year or so sufficient Gibbins bogies were found to re-wheel them.

Work had started on rebuilding the Dungeness line as soon as the Hythe section reopened, and one track was restored as far as Maddieson's Camp by midsummer 1946, enabling special trains to be run for the lucrative camp business. But it soon became clear that so many rails had been damaged that it was not going to be possible to repair both tracks without additional steel. Broken sleepers could be replaced with second-hand standard-gauge ones cut into three, which were readily available, but new or even useful secondhand rail could not be had. A single line only was therefore rebuilt, with some spring points put in at the head of the Dungeness loop. Howey accepted this situation reluctantly, and one motive for the Eaton purchase was to be able to use the materials to relay the second track to Dungeness. But it was found that Heywood's very light 16 lb/yard rail and cast iron sleepers would be unsatisfactory. Although it all reached New Romney, most of the rail ended up as fence posts.

The line was usable again to Dungeness early in 1947, although the barbed wire and scaffolding remained for a year or two longer. It was decided to have a gala reopening ceremony, combined with the railway's official 21st birthday party held a few months early. It so happened that the film comedy duo Laurel and Hardy were in England at the time, playing at the London Palladium, and they agreed to come down and preside at the revels. They wanted no pay; all they asked was that they be brought down in two hired cars, so that if one broke down they could still get back in time for curtain-up. It turned into a tremendous event, with all the fooling around filmed and sent round the world on the newsreels. In the event the hired cars were not needed, since the comedians were taken in hand by the party of Southern Railway officers and steamed back to Charing Cross in an aura of whisky fumes and the SR

Northern Chief at Hythe on a Dymchurch shuttle, July 1947. The first four opens are built on the last surviving set of articulated four-wheelers; following one other open on a 16ft bogie frame, Heywood coaches from Eaton Hall. (*J. C. Flemons*)

General Manager's saloon. This second blast of publicity ensured that the crowds in 1947 were bigger than ever.

Meanwhile, as men were steadily released by the services, Holder set about trying to build up a permanent staff to run the railway. This was never easy; wages were always low, and although it was usually possible to recruit keen young men who dreamed of such a job, as time went on they tended to get married and start families and sheer economic pressure forced them to leave for better pay elsewhere. It needed considerable economic dedication to stay on the railway for more than a few years, and it is surprising all things considered how many men did last for so long. In postwar times they included Jack Hook, the foreman platelayer who rebuilt the Dungeness line; Leslie Thomas and Ralph Kilsby in the workshops, the latter one of several Romney men to die in harness at no great age; Bob Hobbs and above all George Barlow among the drivers. Barlow had been a proof reader on the *Nottingham Journal* before the war, and as an enthusiast had managed to get into the RE Railway Operating Division on joining the army. His adventures on the footplate gave him the fatal itch to remain on it after demobilisation, and Holder took him on in early 1947. After a few weeks he took over No 1 *Green Goddess*, and 30 years later he was still that engine's regular driver, quite possibly a record

length of association between man and machine.

One innovation during 1947 was a daily nonstop train the whole length of the line, named the Bluecoaster Limited. This was more of a prestige than commercial success, though it did not do too badly, and a timing of 45 minutes for the $13\frac{1}{2}$ miles ensured quite an exciting run. Howey, though he did little driving in later years, often worked this train himself, to the disorganisation of the drivers' duty schedules. The staff, however, were in some ways happier to see him on this job than on ordinary stopping trains because at least he would then couple up the brakes, which he did not otherwise always bother with. A pair of special observation saloons, named *Pluto* and *Martello*, were built on 16ft frames to form part of the Bluecoaster, and a supplementary fare charged to travel in them.

Even though passenger business was brisker than ever before, this did not complete the picture. With so much reconstruction going on after the war, there was a great demand for ballast to use in making concrete, and the pits round Lydd, Dungeness, and West Hythe were extremely busy. Howey together with several local businessmen formed a new company, the Romney Marsh Ballast Co Ltd, to exploit the area served by the old WD branch line near Maddieson's Camp. A crusher was installed, a total of 60 four-wheeled 1 cu yd tipping wagons of standard contractors' type but modified for 15in gauge were acquired, and by late summer 1946 the railway was in the freight business in a big way. For the first year or so trainloads of ballast were run through to Hythe, where the pre-war

56

ramp was fitted with an electric winch to draw wagons up the slope, and the delivery hoppers were refurbished; from there it was distributed by road. Business amounted to as much as three or four trainloads a day, which in fact often had to run by night during the summer to keep out of the way of the passenger service. The operation was successful enough technically, apart from minor problems like the occasion when the wet shingle froze solid en route, and the first wagon tipped to discharge at Hythe accompanied its load into the bins, dragging the rest of the rake behind it.

There were also troubles connected with the extremely unsuitable wagons. Their centre of gravity was much too high, and a number of them also had very low-grade wheels prone to shift on the axle. In one case this happened as a loaded train was running through St Mary's Bay station, and the result was an almighty pile-up, with wagons running amok in all directions and great heaps of gravel everywhere. As well as being too high, the wagons were also too wide, and ballast trains could not pass each other at certain points where the double tracks were closer than usual. Apart from all these survivable problems, the traffic brought little profit to the railway since the rate was set at a penny per ton mile, rather a pre-1914 rule-of-thumb main-line charge, and quite uneconomically low for such a short haul.

For these reasons the ballast traffic was fairly short-lived. Had the ex-Eskdale bogie hoppers still been available, it might have been a different story. In the event, it was decided in 1948 to abandon the ballast ramp at Hythe and build a new one in the car park at New Romney; this shortened the length of journey from ten miles each way to two. The following year plans were changed yet again, and a ballast crusher and ramp installed by the lineside a quarter mile south of New Romney station, where they remain, and a 15in gauge siding laid in to serve it.

With all these trains running, the rather war-weary fleet of locomotives needed urgent attention as well. Although mostly operational, several were very run down. *Typhoon* had numerous shrapnel holes in the boiler jacket and *Hurricane* a nasty bulge in the firebox. The only possibility of getting overhauls done quickly was to enlist the aid of the Southern Railway, and have them carried out at Ashford Works. Fortunately O. V. S. Bulleid, the Southern's Chief Mechanical Engineer, had been Gresley's assistant on the LNER before the war, and Holder smoothed the way with Sir Eustace Missenden, the SR General Manager, by arguing that this help would be needed to protect the summer Saturday through-booked traffic from Charing Cross to Dymchurch. *Hercules* went first, followed by *Typhoon* and *Green Goddess*. They had their general repairs alongside some of Bulleid's brand-new streamlined Pacifics; each engine also acquired a new, larger tender at about the same time. Beyond all this, the rusty remains of *Samson* were collected together and sent off to Clifford Edwards & Co in Brighton, and this long-lost machine returned to service in 1947 after nearly 20 years of dereliction. It almost didn't happen; Howey was horrified at the estimate of £2,000 for the rebuild, but Holder insisted that the machine was essential.

The platelayers at Hythe, 1947, on the WD Tractor and a Heywood-type four-wheeler.

Dunrobin arriving at New Romney in 1950, seen on the RH&DR-owned mixed-gauge siding, and posed alongside No 9 *Winston Churchill* and train.

Meanwhile, engine No 9 was renamed *Winston Churchill* in 1948 by the great man's grandson, and went on a trip to Canada, being exhibited in a Toronto department store over the Christmas period. During its absence Howey had slight second thoughts. 'We must have a *Doctor Syn*', he said, and so No 9's discarded nameplates were attached to No 10 and the name *Black Prince* went into limbo.

The Rolls-Royce was still soldiering on, and even though Howey's old petrol-driven thunderbox had failed to survive the war, the army's light four-wheeled locomotive had been taken on instead. The Eaton Railway purchase had included one very solid Simplex tractor, a lineal descendant of some of the early petrol-engined machines which had worked on the military railways in France during the first world war and proved their usefulness there. In spite of its maximum speed of only 10mph, the Simplex was ideally suited to heavy freight work and it took over the ballast trains as soon as they were cut back to New Romney in 1948.

Not everything was plain sailing during those years. The first shock was quite shortly after the start of the 1946 season, when *Southern Maid* collided with a lorry on the level crossing at Eastbridge Road and ended up in the dyke, from which she was rescued by an army team with a mobile crane. The lorry driver, a local man, was killed. This level crossing, because of the lack of visibility between the houses, was quite the worst on the railway, and since that accident a flagman was always posted there. In addition, negotiations with the Ministry and with the local authorities took place to ensure that no new houses would in future be allowed to be built in such a way that they restricted visibility at level crossings so badly.

Another accident befell *Typhoon* early the following year, at a farm crossing near the Prince of Wales. A tractor crossing the lines became stuck because its tyreless driving wheels were smooth steel without spuds or spikes, and slipped when they tried to climb over the rails. The tractor driver did nothing to warn any trains, but just sat gunning the motor and hoping for the best; which, as always, didn't happen. *Typhoon* came round the bend on a down train and ended up on her side, the tractor was split into two parts; fortunately nobody was hurt. Howey and Holder had been on a trip to the north of England that day, and were driving innocently down the A1 next morning when they stopped near Peterborough for a coffee and newspaper. There on the front page was *Typhoon* lying on her side. Howey leapt for the telephone, only to be told by his wife 'Oh, I didn't tell you about it yesterday because I knew you'd be worried. Anyhow, we got the engine back on the line in twenty minutes.'

Apart from the incident at St Mary's Bay, the ballast trains ran fairly smoothly on the main line, though on the gradients of the branch, climbing out of the pit with the load and through the dip under the SR bridge they presented some problems. There were adventures also with wagons getting away on the ramps, several times at Hythe and at least once at New Romney, when a rake got loose, roared past the signalbox and ended in a great heap in the locomotive shed, narrowly missing one member of the staff on the way.

It was putting it a little strongly perhaps for the army to claim that during the war it gave the RH&DR its first professional operating team, but it was no more than the bare truth that in the immediate postwar years it had its first professional management. Howey never had any commercial flair at all, and once he had the outline of what he wanted, always chose the

No 10 *Black Prince* on a down train near Dymchurch in 1948, consisting mainly of 1934 saloons and including a matching van. The bell, a gift from Jumbo Goddard, who drove the engine at the time, was later stolen. (*J. C. Flemons*)

alternative which cost least initially regardless of what might be earned or saved by spending a little more. Over the years, and particularly after his death, this policy cost the railway an enormous amount of money. But of course he never had any reason to take any interest in the commercial side of the business. Hardie had been an excellent day-to-day supervisor and foreman, but no innovator or director. Holder, however, with much help from the publisher Ian Allan, was very active in drumming up extra business by all kinds of publicity and promotions, as well as starting for the first time to sell souvenirs and refreshments to passengers. Howey could never be bothered with all that. The accounts soon showed the effects of all these things. The railway became enormously profitable in the 1946–49 period, and the accumulated deficit which had loaded down the Balance Sheet since the opening was wiped out in 1948 – a considerable achievement. Inflation helped to some extent, of course, though this was very mild indeed compared with recent experience. The 1949 pound was still worth 7s 6d (37½p) in terms of pre-war money.

Holder repeated the idea of a celebrity visit at the beginning of the 1948 season when Tommy Handley, then at the height of his fame as a radio star, visited the railway. But these large publicity strokes were becoming ever more difficult. Apart from any question of diminishing returns, the personalities of stage and screen were beginning to ask fees for appearances of this kind which even a successful RH&DR could not afford. In any case, much of the postwar success was the result of a lot of hard and unexciting work in getting posters and publicity material distributed, coaxing trade out of bus and coach operators, holiday camp proprietors, and so on. One minor triumph was to bury the hatchet with the East Kent Road Car Company. Since 1927 all its buses on the Folkestone to Hythe service had driven past Hythe station empty and without stopping, on the turning circle beyond the official end of the route at Red Lion Square. Holder persuaded them that these buses could stand outside the station where there was plenty of room, plus a cafe for the crews to relax in, and earn extra custom at the same time. As a result every few minutes, until the routes were reorganised in 1976, a double-decker paraded through the middle of Folkestone showing HYTHE LIGHT RAILWAY STATION on its destination blind.

Regular parties were organised to travel on the railway from the holiday camps. One particularly successful contract for a number of years involved special non-stop trains from Maddieson's to Hythe each summer Saturday. A hundred or so campers from London travelled to and from Maddieson's each week by coach, this being of course much cheaper than doing the journey by train all the way. But when Maddieson's tried to get the necessary road service licence to enable special coaches to be operated for these people, the newly nationalised British Railways objected (as they

The Captain's Engine: *Hurricane* at Hythe in a highly polished state, 1949.

were entitled to under the road service licensing laws) and the application was turned down. Ray Maddieson, being something of an individualist, objected strongly to this and was determined to prevent BR from profiting by such obstructionism. The East Kent company operated a coach service from Hythe to London, and he put his campers onto that; special RH&DR trains were laid on to connect.

Yet another new venture was tried in 1947. Colonel Tyrrell, who had purchased Greenly's old bungalow, and had operated a 7½in gauge line some 600yd long on the abandoned RH&DR formation near the locomotive shed since the mid-1930s, had reawakened Howey's old interest in railways of that size, and in 1939 the latter had installed a short 10¼in gauge track, with the small 0–6–0T already mentioned, at Dymchurch. In 1947 he purchased a Bassett-Lowke Royal Scot 4–6–0 of the same gauge from the Marquess of Downshire. Although little used, this machine needed a lot of mechanical improvement. When it had been put to rights Howey looked round for a longer line to run it on. His wife had gone to Australia ahead of him that year, so he was able to bring the Royal Scot into the living room at *Red Tiles* to gloat over it. Once it was installed in the house, temptation overwhelmed him and he

steamed it up, to his great satisfaction but the absolute devastation of carpets, curtains, and furniture. Trouble was avoided by having the house redecorated as a coming-home present for Gladys; meanwhile the locomotive had gone to Hastings, where he built a quarter-mile line along the head of the beach. This was run by the RH&DR for a couple of years, then sold to Ian Allan, and after various changes of ownership still operates. The Royal Scot later went to Oakhill Manor in Somerset and then to the USA. Meanwhile Colonel Tyrrell ran other lines on various sites nearby, one in Folkestone and another for a while on the front at Littlestone, before finally retiring from the business in the late 1950s.

But if the RH&DR's success reflected great credit on Holder, it did not give Howey as much pleasure as it would have done before 1939. Things had changed for him in many ways. His son Tony had not survived the war; he had been a pilot in the Fleet Air Arm, and was flying a transport plane from the Orkneys to Inverness in February 1943 when it was lost with no survivors. His daughter Gloria was in poor health and a constant worry. The postwar years were grim and drab, and he was beginning to grow old. It would be wrong to say that Howey became embittered, but he was no longer a happy man. Even his annual trips to Australia were now a chore.

Currency restrictions barred the route across Canada, and he had to go by sea via Suez. This meant a month of boredom each way in a private suite, relieved only by playing bridge, at which he was admittedly formidable. But it was no substitute for riding across the Rockies on the footplate of a Selkirk 2–10–4.

One further cause of depression was the fact that the Australian pound was no longer linked to the British, and sank in value across the exchanges so that it only purchased 16s (80p) in England. Howey never regarded this as anything but a swindle (not perhaps quite as unsophisticated a viewpoint as all that), and as a result refused to bring any more money out of Australia. The establishment at *Red Tiles* was cut down, and other economies were made. Not to put too fine a point on it, both he and his wife became somewhat miserly. At no time after 1945 was there ever any question of putting more money into the railway. It would have to sink or swim on its own, financially. Fortunately it swam, very buoyantly at first. The houses the company

New Romney station from the air in 1947. In the foreground, *Red Tiles* with the locomotive sheds and works next door; what is now the car park is part of an ex-army stores and part a field; stacks of sleepers for post-war track repairs; and in the distance, the relatively puny SR branch terminus.

owned, Melbourne Villas in New Romney and the old Manager's house at Hythe, were sold and the proceeds used to pay off the mortgage on them, which Howey had taken over from the building society during the war. There were one or two other tax-free benefits in kind – some motoring expenses, and the house heated with railway coal. It was only fair, in a way, that Howey should at last get back something on his investment. Fundamentally, though, he was ageing, and oddly enough, but like a lot of old people, beginning to feel insecure. He did much less driving after 1947, when he was 61, and although the RH&DR was still the main interest of his life he pursued it with less vigour than before the war. One exception was the O gauge model railway exhibition at New Romney, which was established in 1948. Howey took a close interest in this, and spent a lot of time working on it, making much of the scenery himself.

There is a fund of stories about the Howeys' tightness with cash, which became legendary, although they would probably have been horrified to realise it. They range from the mildly malicious, as when Mrs Howey slipped off a chair while changing a light bulb in *Red Tiles* from an extravagant 60 watts to 40, and was in hospital for several weeks, to the quite dreadful. Of the latter a prize example was when George Barlow

Driver of *Green Goddess* for over 30 years, and Operating Manager of the RH&DR until his retirement in 1981, George Barlow, seen for once on a different engine, but still complete with his SNCF engineman's goggles. (*P. C. Hawkins*)

once slipped a disc lifting a weight when working on *Green Goddess*. He was in great pain, and had to be lifted off the engine and helped home, where he was off work for a couple of weeks. During this time he had accepted an invitation to give a lecture about the railway in Leeds; since he did not want to break this engagement the doctor reluctantly strapped him up and sent him north with strict orders to take things easy. When Mrs Howey heard he had gone, she said 'if he's fit to lecture he's fit to work', and refused to make up his sick pay. With treatment like this, it is astonishing that any staff loyalty remained at all, but it did somehow. Possibly one saving grace was that Howey retained a sense of humour. He was capable of telling a story against himself, as when, on one of his driving days, a British Railways engineman came up to him at Hythe and asked what conditions were like, working on the RH&DR 'Oh, very good' replied Howey. 'And the money?' 'Very good as well.' 'That's interesting' said the BR man. 'I'd heard that the owner of this railway was a mean old skinflint.'

One odd might-have-been was in 1948, when Howey contemplated buying the then-closed Festiniog Railway, and went with Holder to Portmadoc to have a look at it; 20 minutes walking round Boston Lodge Works with the FR Manager, dear old lugubrious Robert Evans, was enough. Muttering 'quite impossible', he roared off back to Kent, and the sleeping Festiniog beauty had to wait another six years for Prince Charming. But he had mellowed even to consider the idea. When he visited the break-up sale of the Lynton & Barnstaple in 1935, perhaps the only man at the auction who could have written a cheque for the whole railway as it stood, he had no time for the lovely little Manning Wardle 2–6–2Ts standing round waiting for the chop. 'Dreadful old things with long funnels' was how he described them later.

There was an odd parallel to these cases in Australia around 1957. At that time the 2ft 6in gauge line from Upper Ferntree Gully to Gembrook, a highly scenic affair running through the hills on the outskirts of Melbourne, and actually connecting with the city's suburban electric trains, lay closed and an enthusiast group was endeavouring to reopen it. They took Howey for a ride over some of the line on a motor trolley; he enjoyed himself, thanked them politely, and disappeared without further comment. Perhaps he had noticed that the 2–6–2Ts were not unlike those at Barnstaple. As it happened, the scheme progressed even without his backing, and is now certainly one of the half-dozen most successful steam tourist railways in the world.

Having to contend with such a proprietor, living on the railway as well, meant that things were not easy for Holder, particularly as Howey refused him any salary increase. After three years Holder felt he had had enough and with regret left the railway's service at the end of the 1948 season, resigning as a director and selling his shares the following year. At the beginning of the 1949 season Howey appointed as General Manager Lt-Col R. B. Y. Simpson, DSO, at precisely half Holder's salary.

Simpson had been in the army all his adult life – 31 years in the Durham Light Infantry – and he had only just left it. He took some time to get used to the different way in which things got done in a civilian enterprise. George Barlow still possesses a notice once pinned to the engine shed board at New Romney which began 'Men will parade by the coal heap at 8 a.m. . . .', and in a number of ways Simpson ruffled some feathers at first. But he soon found his feet, and made a solid contribution to the railway's well-being. He was never a railway enthusiast with a flair for publicity and promotion, like Holder, and the

The rebuilt Rolls-Royce shunting at Hythe, with Howey at the throttle, about 1948.

keynote of his policy could best be described as 'sound administration'. Things were set up on a much more regular and professional basis. Holder had moved some way in this direction, since he had seen immediately after the war that Howey's old extravagant prewar ways would have to stop. The railway had to earn its keep; it had therefore to run with the smallest number of staff possible, who would have to double their jobs between winter and summer. Before the war a platelayer was a platelayer and a driver a driver; if there were few trains running, there was no work for drivers, but the track gang soldiered on at full strength even in August. Now the men had to have two different tasks, driving trains during one part of the year while they maintained them, or the track, in the off-season. Although there were still a few volunteer 'slave drivers', some of them veterans of pre-war summers, and a few retired main-line footplatemen who took over an engine for a week or two during the summer peak, the great bulk of the work was now done by permanent full-time staff.

Simpson got to grips with the endless detail of administration and slowly brought it to order. At the other end of New Romney yard, George Barlow set up an equivalent administrative machine in regard to locomotive maintenance, boiler washouts, and drivers' duties, extending it to cope with the routine overhaul of all the coaches each winter. The vacuum brakes continued to work. Mrs Howey now became more involved with the railway than she had been before the war, and in particular took over the management of the Dungeness cafe, and the emptying of the pennies from the locks on the doors of the ladies' lavatories. The Captain presided and oversaw, taking an interest wherever he chose.

The railway continued through these years on the plateau of success where Holder had left it, and after a while it was seen that Simpson's methods kept it there with a minimum of fuss and bother, at least in the short term. There were few changes. One was the sale of the Romney Marsh Ballast Company to a large national quarrying concern in 1951. That was the end of the remaining ballast traffic; the purchasers went over to road transport, the branch line at Maddieson's and the siding to the crushing plant at New Romney were both taken out, and the rolling stock divided between the RH&DR and the newcomers. The latter took the worst vehicles and scrapped them; the 30 or so best ones remained in use for the railway's own requirements, and a dozen still survive.

Simpson was appointed a director of the company in 1950, which made as a rule for smoothness of management during the Howeys' annual Australian journey. One occasion when it did not was when he instituted a pension scheme for the railway's staff in 1951. This was at the time a sensible and benevolent means by which a company could provide a useful benefit for its long-serving staff at relatively small cost, but on her return Mrs Howey was furious and, after

Southern Maid on her side at Eastbridge road, Dymchurch, after the collision in which the driver of the lorry visible was killed, in 1946.

Simpson's departure insisted that the scheme be terminated. She was even angrier when she discovered that under the rules the company's contributions to it had to be paid over to the employees, and fought this bitterly but without success.

The Duke of Sutherland, whom Howey had known as a boy at Eton, died in 1949. One of his ancestral heirlooms was a nice little 0–4–4T named *Dunrobin*, to the slightly morbid

Typhoon on her side near the Prince of Wales in 1947, having collided with the tractor; this is the picture Howey saw in the newspaper.

amusement of a few early Socialists. Built in 1895, this machine had ornate details like a rosewood lining to the cab interior, and had been kept on the Duke's estate near Helmsdale to run errands on the 86-mile line to Inverness whenever required. It had been little used since the 1920s, and the Duchess agreed to sell it for sentimental reasons. Howey had been an old friend and she was sure he would give the engine a good home. It came south, partly under its own power and partly hauled dead in freight trains, Howey and Bob Hobbs taking turns on the footplate, and finally steamed the last few miles to New Romney where a second-hand Nissen hut had been erected to house it at the end of the standard-gauge RH&DR siding. There it stayed for 15 years, boiled and exercised up and down the spur once or twice each summer.

With the abandonment of the idea of using the Eaton materials to relay the second track to Dungeness, Howey became reconciled to leaving this section as a single line. By limiting the number of trains which used it, and keeping the Simplex and the ballast traffic out of the way, it was found that this was quite adequate. More trains could have been run by putting in a passing loop en route, but Howey refused to do this as he felt it might cause problems and misunderstandings, which tend to have dramatic and

All nine engines lined up for the press in 1959, though only *Southern Maid* was in steam, and that concealed *Hercules*; left to right, George Barlow, Ralph Kilsby, Stan Walton and Bill Hart. (*Associated Press*)

undesirable results on a single line. However at times of stress he allowed the rules to be bent and stretched a little, which was just as bad. One day during the height of the 1952 season this had the inevitable result.

The single line was, and is, worked on the staff and ticket system, under which collisions are in principle made impossible by having a wooden train staff. This is labelled with the names of the stations at each end of the single line section to which it applies, and it is a rule that no train may enter that section unless the driver is carrying the train staff on his engine. To cater for the situation where two or more trains have to proceed in the same direction before one comes the other way, this rule is modified to allow a train to proceed provided its driver has been shown the staff, and given a written authority or ticket, signed, dated, and timed, ordering him on, in which case the final train of the series carries the staff. At Dungeness there was an understanding that the circular loop counted as part of the single line, and a driver with a ticket could therefore not leave the station until the train carrying the staff had arrived. On this occasion, a special train was running and things were a little pressed for time, so the driver of the first train was told to leave

Dungeness early and wait to be shown the staff at Britannia Points, where the actual single line began. This would save the time represented by the journey round the loop. Needless to say, when he got to the points he forgot, did what he usually did, and carried on.

The impact was fortunately only mild. One locomotive had actually started to reverse its train when it occurred. *Typhoon* and *Hurricane* both had smashed front bufferbeams, but as the result of an all-night session in the works both were fit to run again next day. But Simpson's military and methodical training made him insist that the incident had serious implications for safety and the only proper course of action was to have a formal inquiry, with statements from all the staff involved, so that the true blame and more important the true weakness in the system which

Coaches, and a four-wheeled luggage truck, telescoped following the Palmarsh collision in 1963.

In preparation for its overhaul at Ashford Works in 1946; *Hercules* in mid-air alongside the brand-new Bulleid pacific 21C119, later 34019 *Bideford*. *(Ian Allan Ltd.)*

had led to the accident could be discovered and put right. Howey took the view, 'oh, we don't want to be bothered with all that'; Simpson insisted, and when he could not get his way, resigned. He was, of course, quite right. Although one has some sympathy with Howey's easy-going approach, safety on a railway in the last resort can only depend on rigid and absolute adherence to set methods, without which there can be no certainty as to how men will act. And without this certainty, danger arises. Howey ultimately received a considerable rocket from the Railway Inspectorate, making just this point.

So finally, for the last 11 years of his life, Howey ran the railway himself. He had no General Manager, and no assistance but that given by his wife, a book-keeper, and when necessary, his solicitor or his accountant. They were in most ways years of slow decline. Certainly that was what happened to the traffic, although it was a very gradual process. These were also the years during which other privately-owned tourist railways began to appear. The Ravenglass & Eskdale was slowly going downhill at the time, for rather similar reasons, and the nationalised Vale of Rheidol seemed to cling to pale life by a very fragile thread. But the Snowdon Mountain remained as prosperous as ever, and meanwhile the first of the preserved railways, Talyllyn,

Festiniog, and Bluebell, began to stir gently in a new way. The Romney still easily outclassed all of them, its annual passenger carryings during the early 1950s exceeding the total of the others added together. But as lines on a graph, they were beginning to converge. The spread of car ownership probably had something to do with it; people were more mobile, and the Romney's relative accessibility from London by rail became less of an advantage. Wales, the Peaks, the Lakes, were now just as easy to reach for a family holiday, and had scenery as well. These new areas began to prosper while the South East declined, though still only slowly. But above all during those years began the relentless government policy, continued by both parties, of subsidising these new holiday districts, including especially their hotels and amenities, to the continuing and cumulative disadvantage of the South and Centre and corresponding benefit of the North and West. Originally intended as a mild corrective to the industrial decline of some of the latter areas, this regional policy grew into an extremely voracious and destructive sacred cow of British politics.

But the RH&DR continued to run pretty efficiently. Dilapidations began to mount, chiefly in buildings, track, and rolling stock, but it was all covered up fairly well by paint and the trains kept time. Howey's last alteration to the railway was in fact the construction of a new paint shop in 1957. About two years before he died, he contemplated selling the railway to Ian Allan, a young man who since his earlier association with the RH&DR had turned his publishing company into a very substantial concern. Allan eventually rejected the idea because he could see the costly problems that were peeping above the horizon, coupled with the shift in tourism away from the railway's catchment area. By the 1970s both he and Holder were deeply involved with the standard-gauge Dart Valley Railway, hauling summer visitors in Devon.

Like any other railway, the Romney continued to record its incidents and individuals. Incidents mainly consisted of level crossing accidents; there was generally about one impressive prang each summer on one or other of the 13 ungated crossings, with damage usually confined to concertinad tinware, the owner of which would emerge dazed from behind his steering wheel with some such comment as 'you must be running late, there's no train due' or 'where did you spring from?' to the startled engine driver. Individuals were many and much more varied and entertaining. One cannot forbear to mention Hammy, who lit fires and swept tubes for several years in the 1950s. He was, and is, a very careful and exact person, who set about tube cleaning with a battery of long rods with steel wire brushes screwed into one end. All boiler tubes were nominally the same, but Hammy knew that some of them had worn larger inside and so a brush five or six thousandths of an inch bigger in diameter was needed to clean them properly. Somebody tried to tease him one day by saying 'Hammy, I think you'll need a bigger brush to do the third tube down in the second row in from the right on the *Maid*.' Hammy thought seriously for a moment, and then replied 'I can't remember that tube needing a bigger brush. But I always use one for the *second* tube down in that row'. He finally resigned from the railway's service in 1958 in some distress, because a relative had inconsiderately left him an estate of £$\frac{3}{4}$ million and he had to go and live in Norfolk to look after it.

Howey's policy remained one of spending as little money as possible, in contrast to prewar days, though he was still prepared to lash out on occasion. One example was in the new paint shop building, which was fitted with underfloor electric heating. This proved so enormously expensive to run that he had it disconnected after receiving the first electricity bill. Another was the reboilering of the locomotives. This began when *Northern Chief* needed a new firebox in 1952, and Barlow persuaded Howey to try the effect of adding superheating. It seemed a considerable success, saving around 10 per cent in coal consumption,

just as it had on the main lines 40 years earlier, and so it was decided to make a clean sweep and fit all the engines with new superheated boilers by Gower of Bedford. This was not strictly essential, though naturally the benefit was felt later; the old boilers, though getting rather long in the tooth, could have been kept going for a long time at some penalty in increasing repairs. But certainly reboilering was the better, if not the most economic, solution. Howey lived to see all the engines dealt with but one; the new boiler for *Doctor Syn* was on hand but not yet fitted when he died.

Superheating remained an economic proposition as long as replacement superheater elements could be obtained cheaply. Unfortunately this depended on other customers using the special steel forgings needed, and most of them, as it happened, were the owners of steam trawlers. With the extinction of ships of that sort in recent years, the cost of new elements has skyrocketed and it is doubtful whether superheating saves the railway money any longer in the 1980s. But all this lay far in the future.

Even if he unbelted for the locomotives, Howey spent very little on coaches after the 1940s. The old Clayton Pullmans soldiered on, getting pretty tatty (they retained their original 1929 upholstery into the 1970s) but since they were solidly built they took a long time to fall to pieces. The Hythe saloons, however, were not nearly so substantial and during the 1950s they deteriorated rather quickly, as did the postwar coaches on the ex-Eskdale ballast frames. The cheapest possible softwood and hardboard bodies were erected on both types of frame in replacement, and a further economy made in some cases by abolishing doors, so creating a new type of semi-open coach. Where doors were retained, sliding instead of hinged ones were used to reduce repair costs, though this change was rather a success. Many passengers found them easier to manage. They had never been in a traditional slam-door BR compartment, and did not know how to get out by lowering the window first and using the outside door handle.

But another change, replacing cushioned seats with hard slats, may have saved money but was disastrous for both comfort and public relations. Even the only wholly new coaches built after 1950 had slat seats. These were six 16-seat saloons built in 1962 on eight new 20ft all-welded frames by Gower of Bedford (the two remaining frames were left unbodied at Howey's death). New bogies (without brakes) were obtained from Hudson of Leeds. Howey seldom travelled on the railway in

For a long time the only convenient place for transferring heavy loads from rail to road was St Mary's Bay station, where the platforms ran directly off the level crossing. In October 1955 two boilers are sent away for repair, loaded by a portable gantry. In fact both boilers were condemned and replaced with new ones. (*G. A. Barlow*)

his last years, but for some reason rode in one of these flimsy new coaches a few weeks before he died and was so appalled by its lack of comfort that he said 'we must do something about this'. But he never had time to.

He sometimes made sudden irrational decisions on the spur of the moment. One day he saw an engine go by with the brakes dragging on one tender wheel. Instantly he ordered the tender brakes to be removed, which left some locomotives, notably the 4–8–2s, with practically no brake power at all. There was a crossover leaving New Romney station which allowed trains to depart from the old high level platforms and still gain access to the up line for Hythe. He felt a bump once going over this and the next morning, which happened to be August Bank Holiday, he ordered it to be taken out at once. Similarly, the Rolls-Royce locomotive was scrapped in 1961 when it needed some repairs; it was a serious loss as it had been a useful machine.

One rather complicated, and at least from other parties' point of view unsatisfactory, hobby of Howey's was planning new locomotives. He had actually taken this up before the war, to the point of commissioning a four-cylinder LMS Princess Royal Pacific from H. C. S. Bullock of Farnborough. Unfortunately Bullock had bitten off more than he could chew with such a large job, and got into such a serious financial and

emotional pickle over it that he committed suicide. Howey drove across to Farnborough as soon as he heard the news and extracted the completed parts, plus the $10\frac{1}{4}$in gauge 0–6–0T already mentioned, from the widow in settlement of the money he had paid on account. The postwar exercises were less disastrous but not much more constructive. The chief victim was H. Holcroft, Assistant CME of the Southern Railway, who prepared a full set of working drawings for a neat, if rather starkly modern, 2–8–2 and an outline proposal for an enormous three-cylinder 4–8–4. He never got paid for the considerable amount of work involved. Howey unrolled the general arrangement drawing of the 2–8–2, said 'what an ugly brute', and that was that. Slightly luckier was Ian Hunter, a consulting engineer who prepared outlines for another 4–8–4 and an American-style duplex-drive 4–4–4–4. Nothing happened there either, but at least he designed and got paid for the new standard boilers, designed to fit all nine locomotives.

Perhaps the luckiest escape was David Curwen's. Curwen is a quiet sort, of the butter-not-melting-in-the-mouth type, with great charm and, when necessary, guile. Howey invited him to New Romney on a couple of occasions to talk about a new engine. Knowing the score, Curwen would carry on for hours over lunch with miniature railway reminiscences and generalities, tactfully parrying any attempt to turn the conversation in more concrete directions, and when Howey finally nodded off to sleep in mid-afternoon, he would make his excuses to Gladys and tiptoe away.

To the end of his life Howey regretted the failure of his and Zborowski's plans for the

Ravenglass & Eskdale. The two men had undoubtedly had the resources, and the ability to obtain the legal power, to carry out their proposed extension from Dalegarth under Hardknott and Wrynose passes to Ambleside, on Lake Windermere, and if built this would have been an absolute world-beater of a railway, a miniature version of the crossing of the Alps or the Rockies. But all foundered on Brocklebank's refusal to sell, coupled with Zborowski's untimely death. The irony there was that Zborowski had intended the Monza event to be his last race, after which he would concentrate on the project; and Brocklebank might well have come round. Even in the 1950s, Howey would sometimes appear unannounced at Ravenglass and sit silently on the wall watching; which used to upset Harry Hilton, the Manager. Occasionally somebody would draw him into conversation, and he would make unflattering, but then quite justified, comparisons between Romney and Eskdale equipment, and politely regret what might have been.

The very last spell of driving Howey did was for a few days in the summer of 1957, when he was 70, during a period when things were very tight. He had built himself a summerhouse near the turntable at New Romney, where he could sit and read and watch the trains go by; and later on another one, glassed in to protect him from the cold winds. He stepped onto one of his engines only once again. A few days before he died, George Barlow saw him looking wistfully at *Green Goddess*, and on an impulse invited him to take it over. It was just what Howey had wanted, in a way; but when he backed onto the train he misjudged his braking and hit the coaches an awful wallop. He handed the engine back, saying sadly 'I seem to have lost my touch'.

He still had unpredictable bursts of energy, and might set off early one morning just to watch the Flying Scotsman leave King's Cross at 10am, then turn straight round and come home. He always liked to have someone with him on these trips, a kindred spirit like Barlow or one of his son's old friends, 'Jumbo' Goddard, a considerable character in his own right. Goddard had known Zborowski, and did a lot of driving on the RH&DR after the war, but if anything he had an even greater interest in classic cars and sailing. In his fifties he was the oldest crew member of the replica *Mayflower* on her transatlantic voyage.

Howey had a jungle-telegraph-like sense for what was happening on the railway behind his back. There was one famous occasion when a driver was using the steam lance to blow his

superheater tubes clear outside the locomotive shed, a process which causes a brief but spectacular eruption of black soot. The wind was fresh that day and bore it all down over the newly hung washing on the *Red Tiles* line. Gladys Howey saw this happen, stormed out of the house, and gave the driver a piece of her mind. As she steamed back indoors, like the little man with the umbrella at the other entrance of one of those comic toy house barometers, Howey emerged from the French windows at the other end of *Red Tiles* and quietly told the driver 'never mind the laundry; you keep your flues clean'.

Yet this sixth sense began to fail at the end. The double track between Hythe and New Romney had always been worked by telephone block, in which safe working depends on the proper following of the rules. Signalmen at Hythe, Dymchurch, and New Romney each have a train register. When a train leaves one station, its departure is reported by telephone to the next station and both signalmen note it, with the engine number and time, in their registers. The first may then not despatch another train in the same direction until the receiving station has reported back that the first train has duly arrived, with number and time, and this message is again recorded in both registers. After a while there came a signalman at Hythe who saw no point in all this palaver. If the management wanted a train register they could have one, but he would fill it in at the start of the day when things were quiet so he would not have to bother with it when he was busy. Unless he was found out first, it was thus only a matter of time before his bomb went off, and it finally did on 3 June 1963.

Hercules had been going badly that day for a very odd reason. The needle of its pressure gauge was loose on its spindle, and as a result the gauge was giving a high reading whose error was slowly increasing. To the young driver this looked most alarming; boiler pressure was apparently far too high and yet the safety valves were not lifting. He called the fitter, Ralph Kilsby, who failed to spot the unusual defect, but instead used the special spanner to ease the safety valve springs so that they did lift at what the gauge said was the right pressure. All kinds of trouble followed, with a strangely listless locomotive and dragging brakes on the train. The driver made it, with difficulty, to Hythe, but on the return journey, running late already, stalled on the curve just beyond the Prince of Wales bridge, just as the Hythe signalman who saw no point in fussy rules sent off the following train as if the line was clear.

The Captain looks on as *Hercules* shunts at New Romney.

Fortunately the second driver had enough warning to apply the brakes just before the collision, but even so 22 passengers were sent to hospital for repairs and most of the coaches on both trains were badly damaged. It was a thoroughly discreditable accident, and it must have shaken Howey. He carried on without comment, but later that summer got steadily weaker. He still drove his Jaguar with skill and judgment, as impressively as ever, and just as fast; he drove at 100mph for the last time on a trip up to London that August. But his passenger sometimes had to find bottom gear for him since he no longer had the strength to force the lever through the gate himself. He died in his sleep on 8 September 1963. His ashes are buried in the station yard at New Romney, in the ornamental rockery opposite the signal box.

A year or so later the solicitors who were handling his Australian affairs had reckoned the value of his Melbourne estate up to six million pounds, and were still counting. Gladys Howey died in 1974; their daughter Gloria had gone a few years earlier. No attempt had been made to minimise the impact of death duties, which after two repeated cuts was devastating; a fraction of what it had been, the Howey estate in Melbourne was liquidated in the mid-1970s. The main beneficiaries were the Australian and British governments. Howey Place remains, with the Presgrave Building close by; now slightly run-down, both look as if demolition and rebuilding are not far off. There may soon be no concrete reminder of Henry Howey's lucky bid in that auction, over 140 years ago, at any rate in Melbourne.

Howey and the $10\frac{1}{4}$in Royal Scot in the sitting room at *Red Tiles*, before he gave way to temptation or had to replace the curtains.

7
Under New Managements

At the time he died, Captain Howey owned 48,747 of the 51,000 issued shares of the Romney, Hythe & Dymchurch Light Railway Company, plus his house *Red Tiles*, but no other property in the area. Gladys Howey, to whom everything was left, had no wish to continue to live at New Romney and soon moved permanently back to London, making an occasional day trip to visit old friends in the area. She put the railway on the market, and although it is not every day that such a thing comes onto the books, the local estate agent in New Romney managed to sell it for her, together with the house. The buyers, who took possession on 1 July 1964, were S. H. Collins and J. E. Scatcherd, two retired bankers who had come to live in the district and felt that the RH&DR would do very nicely to provide an interesting little business to keep them occupied. Collins was the active partner, who soon moved into *Red Tiles* with his wife and made the railway a full-time job. However, neither man was in the least sentimental about it nor any kind of railway enthusiast, and their approach to running it was very different indeed from Howey's.

Viewed as a commercial proposition and in particular as seen from an examination of its accounts, the railway had certain great strengths and possibilities. One was that its revenue was almost exclusively in cash. All those problems of credit control, invoicing, and bad debts so familiar to bankers were almost completely absent. Equally obvious were the facts that the company had traded profitably for a long time, even though Howey had hardly bothered to try, and that it would not be difficult to improve the results by applying a bit of commercial thinking. Finally, there was the substantial guarantee of a unique and world-famous collection of assets in the locomotives and rolling stock, plus some useful freehold land. Mrs Howey was happy to accept a price of £1 for each of her shares, and so for an outlay of around £50,000 in 1964 money the partners obtained an undertaking which had cost Howey more than double that 40 years

earlier. It was also debt-free; Howey had had a horror of running an overdraft, and the company sat each autumn on a pile of cash large enough to see it through until the following summer. It all looked completely gilt-edged; the weaknesses of the situation were not at all easy to see. They were, however, there.

Collins made one of the drivers, Peter Catt, Manager of the railway and left day-to-day running largely to him. Catt was a local man, still in his thirties, who had become fascinated by the railway as a boy and started working for it as soon as he left school. Although they came from such different backgrounds, a close friendship grew up between the two men, which certainly made life easier. Nobody at New Romney seems able to remember an occasion when Collins actually rode on one of his trains, let alone one of his engines, but he soon got a very good idea of what was going on and what made everybody tick, and was generally liked and respected. He also did some good things for the railway.

One notably overdue improvement was to build a cafeteria at New Romney station, filling a long-felt want and setting up a profitable new area of trading at the same time. Sheer necessity had forced Howey to operate the cafe at Dungeness, simply because hearing the complaints of parched and famished passengers on all those acres of desert shingle was an even bigger bore than having to put up with the tedium of selling them cups of tea, and the fact that the Dungeness cafe always did well financially was of little interest to him. But even Holder had not been able to set up anything better at New Romney than a small caravan or kiosk selling tea and biscuits, and those who wanted more had to look elsewhere. Unfortunately the building erected at New Romney, next to the Model Exhibition and on the roof of the old concrete carriage shed, was an exceedingly cheap and flimsy one.

Another improvement owed more perhaps to Peter Catt. New Romney station had always been illogically laid out and difficult to work ever since the construction of the Dungeness extension and destruction of the original terminus in 1928. There were two particular nonsenses. One was that any train arriving from Hythe and terminating at New Romney, unless it was very short and so able to use the surviving half of the old station, blocked itself in; this was because the points leading to the engine shed and turntable were in the middle of the down main platform, and so under the middle of the train. Much complex shunting through the blind tunnels under Littlestone Road resulted in order to release the locomotive. The other nonsense was that the up main platform, the only one which could be reached by a train arriving from Dungeness, was much too short, and also sited well away from the others, which was confusing in itself. If the locomotive stopped by the water column, the rear half of most up trains stretched back short of the platform; and what was worse, stood close to a concrete wall on the platform side so that people were forced to get in and out by standing on the down main line, an extremely undesirable situation. As a non-railwayman Collins could not really see the point of doing anything to remove the first difficulty, but as a practical businessman and banker the risks of the second struck him very forcibly, and he quickly carried out another long overdue and very sensible improvement by demolishing the offending concrete wall and extending the up main platform back towards Littlestone Road, so that was now long enough for any likely train. At the same time, the footbridge giving access to it was moved to a logical position near the station entrance.

In other matters Collins and Scatcherd were content to let things roll on as they had for so long. Both men were in their sixties, and could not expect to control the railway for more than a few years. Neither lacked funds and so drawing profits or dividends from it was of no interest to them. Their concern was the perfectly understandable one that they or their legatees should be able to sell the railway again in due course, at a good price and in a tax-efficient manner.

This meant that they were interested in reducing costs and increasing revenue first, and in spending money to ensure the long-term future of the business second. The first would have a direct effect, by increasing apparent profitability, on the price they might expect to obtain on selling; the second only an indirect effect, and at that one not easy to define. One example of the result of this sort of policy can be seen in what the platelaying gang were put to in the winter. The railway owned something over 23 miles of track, laid on around 64,000 sleepers. Originally these sleepers were of new treated softwood, which could be expected to decay at such a rate that some would need replacing after 20 years or less, and a few might last for 50 years or more, but with an average life of between 30 and 40 years. Thus by the 1950s and 1960s it might be expected that each winter an average of about 2,000 sleepers would have to be replaced. True to his postwar policy of choosing the cheapest possible alternative regardless of long-term overall cost, Howey had decided to use second-hand British Railways main line sleepers cut in three for renewals; but since these timbers had already been in use for 15–20 years their remaining life was correspondingly reduced and so the theoretical annual renewal requirement for the RH&DR steadily rose to around 3,500. One of the standard means by which railway managements traditionally pull in their belts during lean years is to reduce the number of sleepers replaced; this can be done without any real harm for a few years, and without serious harm for longer than that, provided the leeway is eventually made up. Since the cost of sleeper renewals is a very significant item in any railway's budget, any cut in the rate of renewal has a considerable effect on the profit-and-loss account, and up to a point this is a useful and legitimate management tool. Collins adopted it, and went further. Once the winter's allotment of new sleepers was into the road, the gang was sent out with a tractor and trailer selling the rotten old timbers for firewood. They made rather bad firewood and fetched so low a price that the exercise did not pay the gang's wages; but still, it brought in something, and if they had spent their time on other track maintenance work the whole of their wages would have been a charge against profits. In the short term, and in a crisis, fine; in the long term, a hell of a way to run a railway.

One asset which was very promptly turned into cash was the Duke of Sutherland's engine. *Dunrobin* had been a sentimental indulgence on Howey's part, and spending nearly all the time locked in its shed with the Duke's private coach it earned little for the railway. Collins sold it as soon as he could, to an operator in British Columbia, who has given it a good home. By now it has probably run more miles in Canada than it ever did in Britain. But the Sutherland family were indignant, and wrote angrily that if they had ever dreamt the locomotive would leave the country they would never have sold it. Too late.

But meanwhile the 15in gauge trains still ran, the crowds were happy, and the paint still sparkled. Collins was a likeable character, and so was Peter Catt. Collins was also acute. One of his party tricks was to walk along the path from *Red Tiles* to the office in mid-morning, just as the first train of the day arrived from Hythe; judging the number of passengers on it with a flick of the eye, he could usually assess the day's takings to within ten pounds or so. He also did quite a lot of practical work on the railway, being something of a do-it-yourself fanatic; with Peter Catt he made most of the tables for the new cafe, and he spent a lot of time repairing carriages. Perhaps the standard of some of the bodywork repairs was not beyond criticism, though doing anything to keep the cheap and nasty postwar bodies going was not easy. Coach sides might begin to flap in the breeze because the wooden solebars to which they were attached were rotten, but with a couple of dozen six-inch nails and a lick of paint it was usually possible to send the vehicle out again. Some of the larger holes, where rotten timber had fallen away, were filled with plastic wood, or rolled-up newspaper and cotton waste, with hardboard nailed on top to take the paint.

Ultimately, of course, more radical repairs were needed, beyond the skill of any member of the staff; as for instance when side panels became detached at the top as well as the bottom, or passengers fell through the seats or put their feet through the floor. One by one, coaches with ailments of this sort were shunted away out of sight under the Model Exhibition at New Romney, and Collins and Scatcherd began to wonder whether the time was coming when they should sell these problems, together with the railway, to somebody else. This calculation was brought a good deal closer when it was felt prudent to get a consulting engineer, P. R. Harmer, to report on the state of the railway's bridges, starting with the Duke of York's. Howey had never seen any need to take advice of this kind, nor had he spent money on scaling and painting the steelwork. So it was perhaps not too surprising that the consultant's report, in early 1967, was not a good one. The bridge was condemned outright and its replacement at the earliest opportunity strongly recommended. Collins accepted this, and a contract was let for the work to be carried out the following winter. Meanwhile matters took another turn.

A group of individuals, mostly living in Folkestone, organized by D. B. Lye and Anthony Record, had recently done quite well with an investment in a pirate radio station. They were looking round for some other local business proposition, and began to contemplate the RH&DR. Legend has it that Anthony Record happened to lean over the wall at New Romney station one August afternoon, just as a well-filled train arrived from Hythe, and decided that he had discovered a gold mine. This is quite an appealing addition to the store of Romney legends, so let it stand. During the following months, the matter was discussed at some length with Collins and Scatcherd, and on 31 May 1968 the deal was concluded; 21 members of the group, including Lye and Record, individually purchased a total of 44,628 shares from Collins and Scatcherd. Collins retained 4,670 himself, and the remaining 1,702 were still held by the minority shareholders of Howey's day. Collins remained a director of the railway company, succeeded as Chairman the following October by Lye; the other members of the new board were Major G. St. G. Stedall and

A hole in the road: new foundations under way for the new Willop Bridge, 1969. (*P. C. Hawkins*)

Installing the sleepers on top of the new girders; the new bridge, or rather twin bridges, at The Willop, 1969. (*P. C. Hawkins*)

First across: *Winston Churchill* tests the new span at The Willop, 1969. Part of the drunken abutment for the old bridge remains in the foreground. (*P. C. Hawkins*)

D. H. Cadman. At the same time, the railway company purchased *Red Tiles*, which Collins continued to occupy until October, while Collins lent the railway company £10,000 to help its cash position.

One factor which had helped persuade Collins that the time had come to sell was the sudden death of Peter Catt at New Romney that spring; Collins had come to rely on him greatly, and was considerably shaken by the event. The new owners appointed a new General Manager in Peter Hawkins, who took up his position during the summer of 1968.

Meanwhile the work of rebuilding the Duke of York's Bridge was in progress. During the winter break the old girders were cut down and sold for scrap. Massive new steel joists were assembled at New Romney station and taken by rail to the

General Manager with shovel: Peter Hawkins lending a hand after No 9 split the points at Hythe, August Bank Holiday 1969. The service was maintained using the remaining two unblocked platforms. (*T. R. S. Miller*)

bridge site, where they were lowered by a mobile crane onto new abutments with deeper foundations, then welded into a single structure. As Easter and the recommencement of train running drew closer, this awful gap remained in the middle of the railway, but in fact the job was finished and track relaid across the water the day before the first train of the season was due to run. As Catt had earlier suggested, the new bridge was renamed Collins Bridge.

The new owners started with a clear determination to set the railway to rights. One of their first acts was to commission P. R. Harmer to survey all the other underline bridges, but when his preliminary report was received a few months later it came as a very rude shock indeed. Of the six, only two were given a clean bill of health; three were declared to need early or very early attention, and one was considered actually dangerous. His full report, received a few weeks later, was even worse.

The details given by Harmer are quite scarifying, and worth quoting. The point was made that although some of the bridges could in theory be repaired, such heavy work was needed that 'it would represent quite a large percentage of the cost of reconstructing the bridges and would only extend their working lives for a short period'. Further, 'the condition of the bridges referred to is in my opinion largely due to complete lack of maintenance. Even a single annual coat of bituminous paint would have greatly reduced corrosion.'

The worst bridge was Hoorns, between Dymchurch and Burmarsh Road, This was composed of three 14in × 6in rolled steel joists spanning a gap of some 22ft between the concrete abutments, in which the ends of the girders were embedded. They had been reinforced by steel

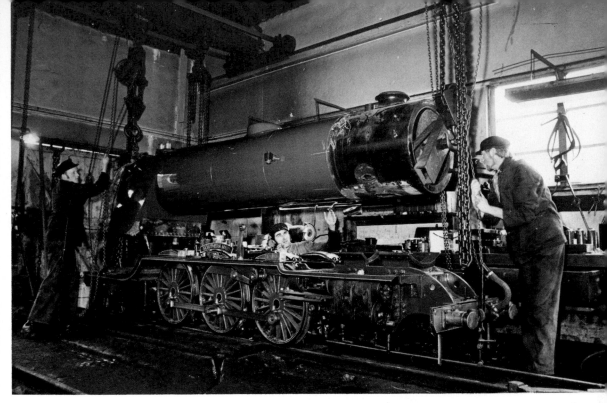

Southern Maid's boiler is lifted, the first overhaul for 10 years. New Romney Erecting Shop, 1969. Left to right: A. R. W. Crowhurst, Barrie Clark, Cyril Carter. (*Associated Press*)

plates riveted top and bottom to increase the effective width of each girder from 6in to 10in; the rails were carried by long timbers laid directly across the top flanges of the girders. One disadvantage of the three-girder construction of this and one other bridge (Carey's) was that the middle girder had to be able to carry a double load, should two locomotives, one on each track, occupy the bridge at the same time. These three girders were in an appalling state, the reinforcing plates in places completely eaten away by rust, and the webs of the main joists badly corroded. There was also considerable damage by shrapnel from a near miss bomb during the war, which had cut right through the steel. Finally, the foundations were inadequate, being founded only about 6in below the bed of the stream.

Carey's Bridge, of 24ft 3in span, was similarly built of three RSJs, though these were of 18in × 6in section and so rather stronger, and had not suffered bomb damage. But because of heavy corrosion, the remaining metal of the girders where they met the concrete was being stressed at the limit of safety and so no repairs could extend the life of the bridge for very long.

Golden Sands Bridge, of 37ft span, was built of four 20in × 7½in RSJs but even so corrosion and neglect had taken the same course as at Carey's, with the same result. Much worse, the bridge had been considerably weakened by notches having been cut in the top flanges of the girders, to take bolts which secured the sleepers.

The fourth dubious bridge, at the Willop, of 40ft span, was quite different from the others. It was supported by four RSJs, three 20in × 7½in and one 24in × 7½in (the difference in sizes reflecting the fact that Greenly had purchased a job lot of second-hand girders in 1926), but these carried a steel trough decking which held some five tons of gravel and ash ballast in which the track was laid. All the steel was massively corroded, and the bridge looked in an appalling state because the foundations had moved, causing the decking to tilt and twist very noticeably. The reason for this movement was evident enough, since it was possible to drive an iron bar by hand into the soft mud below the foundations and above the water on each side of the gap. As each train went over, a shower of small pebbles and flakes of rust fell into the water. As a final and minor blemish, the trough decking was not wide enough to allow the two tracks to be laid the proper distance apart, so that the clearance between two passenger trains passing on the bridge was less than the regulation 2ft, while two ballast trains passing would have actually collided.

Open Joint: a medium-size specimen. This was a common sight for the morning inspection after a cold night, on double track sections. As the fishbolts snapped, the rails would jump apart by anything up to 2ft. (*A. R. W. Crowhurst*)

It was some small comfort that after this devastating report, Harmer passed the other bridges as fit. Collins Bridge, being brand new, was fine; Dymchurch and Botolphs, each of about 35ft span and four-girder construction with open timber decking, were not too bad because their 20in × 7½in girders were reasonably sound, even showing signs of paint. The fact that these were the only two bridges where any paint might have been noticed by people passing on the public highway was not commented on. In addition, some work had been done to strengthen the abutments at Botolphs by the Southern Water Authority when it deepened the New Cut.

The new owners of the railway bit the bullet, and during the next three winters, 1968–71, all four condemned bridges were completely rebuilt with new steel on new, deep, concrete foundations. The same very simple type of bridge was installed in each case, with track laid straight onto the top flanges of the four main girders, but the detail of the design was enormously better than the original, with proper bracing welded into the structure and the steelwork bolted onto the top of the reinforced concrete foundations, thus avoiding the inevitable rust-trap caused whenever steel is embedded into cement. Needless to say, these works cost a substantial amount of money.

But they did not exhaust the list of improvements which the new management began to tackle. On the engineering side, these included a number of important items. There was, for instance, absolutely no stock of spare rail for track repairs, and sidings (whose rails tended to be pretty diseased anyhow) were having to be lifted to keep the main lines usable. With some difficulty, a supply of good second-hand 30 lb/yard rail, salvaged from the abandoned Sierra Leone Government Railway, was located and enough for about half a mile of track purchased.

A local builder put bodies on the remaining two Gower coach frames of the 1962 batch, which were still in store unused, and to tackle the problem of repairs Hawkins recruited a skilled coachbuilder, Eddie Allchin, who had previously worked for London Transport. But once he started repairing, he found that when he had finished cutting away the rotten wood there was very little of the old coach left, and so the policy soon had to change to one of building completely new bodies.

A similar problem was mounting up in the locomotive department, and the need for a new approach there was recognised. It had to start by rebuilding and re-roofing the original Jackson, Rigby machine shop, which for over 40 years had been used as a gigantic store-cum-junk heap. There had to be a massacre; it meant getting rid of all kinds of curious antiquities, such as sets of Heywood's original patterns for great varieties of cast-iron objects from driving wheels to door stoppers, and numberless early Greenly relics. Out they all went to make space, and in came machine tools, lathes and mills and planers, to allow the railway to carry out its own heavy mechanical repairs once more. To take charge in this department a new Chief Engineer, A. R. W. Crowhurst, was appointed. In 1969 the first full-scale locomotive overhaul of the new regime was commenced, on *Southern Maid*. This was the first occasion for over seven years on which any pair of wheels had been taken out of an engine for any reason. Things had been at a very low ebb.

The new owners had started off very energetically, but as they proceeded and became more and more aware of the scale of the problem, they began to get nervous; and not without reason. After all, they were not any sentimental bunch of puffer-nutters. They had regarded the railway as a commercial proposition, which obviously had to be in a good state of repair but which equally obviously had to pay them a return on their money. As a matter of principle, they decided that the company must pay dividends, and 4 per cent was in fact paid for each of the years 1966–70 inclusive. The total cost of these payments, £10,200, was fairly insignificant beside the amount of money spent on renovations; the problem was, there did not seem to be any end to the repairs list. Things got worse all the time, with further unwelcome discoveries. A great deal of effort went into increasing revenue, by advertising and promotions of every kind, and by expanding the souvenir-sales side of the business, but this was obviously not going to be enough. Certain members of the group worked out schemes of improvement, but most were out of reach financially.

The next step was to consider shortening the railway, which in theory made a lot of sense. Only a minority of passengers travelled all the way; sale of land and scrap rail would fund the renovation of the rest. But the problem was, where to chop? Alternatives studied included closing New Romney to Dungeness, or even New Romney to Hythe and keeping Dungeness; shifting the works and depot to land at the School Journey Centre site (ex Duke of York's Camp) at St Mary's Bay and running only from there to Hythe; keeping Hythe to Dymchurch only; and closing everything except the first two miles out of Hythe and running that non-stop with a return loop near Botolph's Bridge Road. The Hythe to Dymchurch option seemed most promising, as some vacant land near the sea wall just west of the village was available and this would make a most attractive terminus; this site was actually purchased. But on closer study every one of the alternatives had to be rejected for one reason or another, and it finally had to be admitted that, poor as the prospects were for the future of the whole railway, the chances of survival of any amputated stump of it were worse. During 1969 the idea was considered of moving the whole concern to South Devon, occupying the line from Goodrington to Kingswear, which BR was about to close. But finance was a problem and ultimately the Dart Valley Railway made a pre-emptive move and got in first.

It is hardly too much to say that the group were ultimately driven to their wits' end, and after several abortive attempts to sell the railway were reduced by summer 1971 to announcing that they saw no possibility of keeping it going and therefore intended to close it. One acute difficulty

The opposite problem to the open joint was the buckle, experienced on a double line on hot days at the approach to a fixed point such as a level crossing. *Green Goddess* negotiating (dead slow but successfully) a smallish buckle near Burmarsh Road in 1977. (*D. Songhurst*)

triggering this decision was that the bank had just noticed the fact that the company's borrowing powers were limited by the Light Railway Order to what was now a wholly inadequate £17,000; since the overdraft was much larger than that they began to emit shrill cries of alarm.

Naturally the announcement created an uproar. There was a considerable amount of fuss in the local and indeed the national press, and much general resistance to the idea, with public meetings, overflow crowds blocking Hythe High Street, and so on. As Chairman of the company, David Lye had to take a great deal of stick, and as always on these occasions out of every hole and hedgerow crept individuals who knew very much better than anyone else how the RH&DR, or indeed any other railway, ought to be run. Nor was it a happy time for the railway's staff. But to a certain degree the situation was slightly contrived. The threat to close down was no doubt genuine enough, but Lye knew that it was also the only thing that would induce a group of reluctant purchasers to bid for the railway.

Richard North, the director of a firm of engineers in Glasgow, had got to know the RH&DR during the 1960s, and had become

Retyring a locomotive bogie wheel, RH&DR style. The new tyre is spun at the end of a wire while heated in a gas flame so that, when expanded, it will fit easily over the cold wheel centre below.

aware of its problems while riding, as he did a great deal, on its engines. He soon realised that his own resources were far too small, but he felt that it should be possible to form a group of several dozen well-to-do railway enthusiasts who between them could afford to step into Howey's shoes and keep the thing going. One problem was that a new company would have to be formed, and that while

Installing the third layout at New Romney, winter 1973/4. The frame of the new train shed starts to go up after the third track through the platforms is completed (on the right). The original platform level is shown by the higher ground further to the right. (*A. R. W. Crowhurst*)

the law restricted the number of members of a private company to 50, the legal difficulties of setting up a small public company were indescribable. During 1969 and 1970 North tried to get such a group together, but failed until two things happened. One was Lye's threat to close down; the other was that he managed to recruit W. H. McAlpine, a member of the family controlling the well-known firm of contractors, who was a keen railway enthusiast. Bill McAlpine had already turned down the idea of buying the railway himself, but he agreed to lead the group North had formed, and put a great deal of effort into recruiting more support. Because the number of backers had to be limited to 50 at maximum, each was asked to find at least £1,000.

The possibility of saving the railway grew. Lye drove a hard bargain, having his clients' interests at stake as well as his own, but ultimately success was achieved and on 14 February 1972 the railway changed hands again. This time the corporate structure was a little more complicated. The new owners formed a private company, RH&D Light Railway Holding Co Ltd, which actually purchased the railway, or to be exact an eventual total of 50,447 of the 51,000 shares, at £2.12 per share. The Holding Company was in turn financed by its members, numbering 32 at the start, with others joining later. As a temporary arrangement, each loaned money interest-free to the Holding Company, receiving only a nominal shareholding.

The original railway company continued to exist, and in fact to operate the business. The directors of each company were the same; Bill

Shortage of operable coaches led to some slightly unconventional uses in the early 1970s.

McAlpine as Chairman, Sir Gerald Glover as Vice-Chairman, R. A. North, J. B. Hollingsworth, and the author as Managing Director. W. J. Germing and C. R. C. Aston joined each Board a while later. Peter Hawkins remained as General Manager. But apart from the changed personalities, the fundamental change was one of motivation. Since 1964 the railway's owners had looked primarily for a return on their investment (and had ultimately obtained one); after 1972 their fundamental objective was to restore, maintain, and develop the railway in line with Howey's and Zborowski's original vision.

Since February 1972 the history of the railway has been a continuing one (with some repeats of previous scenarios), and perhaps as one so closely concerned with it, the author is not the right historian. But it seems worth while trying to bring the story up to date, at least in outline.

The most pressing problems the new directorate faced were mechanical ones. The civil engineering side had had enough first aid for the time being, but this was far from being the case with locomotives and above all coaches. During 1970 and 1971 so many coaches had been unserviceable that revenue had been lost at times because there was simply no room on the trains. Allchin and his assistant Bill Allard were building new coaches as fast as they could, and were currently producing an improved version of the 1946 16ft toastrack opens as the quickest and cheapest way of providing new seats. But of the 79

coaches on the books, no fewer than 21 had to be condemned outright during the first year and moderate to heavy repairs were needed to another 30. It was clearly essential in February 1972 to get as many vehicles as possible on the rails, however bodged and temporary the work had to be, and there was a final and king-sized orgy with six-inch nails, strange metal strapping pieces, and the like. But things did not end with these body problems. Many of the coach wheels were so badly worn that they could no longer be turned up to the correct profile in the lathe because there was not enough metal left on the tread. Nearly all were about 40 years old, but even worse were the new wheels which had been purchased in 1962 for the eight Gower frames. Though far from worn out, these were extremely low grade castings, full of soft spots and blowholes; in one case, when a length of wire was pushed inquisitively down a hole which had appeared in the tread, no bottom whatever was found and it eventually emerged from another hole right across the diameter of the wheel. The list of other defects was a long one, and included a great deterioration of the vacuum brakes.

New wheels were obviously needed right away, and a hundred castings were ordered at once; several hundred more followed during the next couple of years. But taking a longer-term look at the problem certain changes of policy were indicated. First of all, cheap coach bodies were obviously no economy. Some of the 1962 batch had already fallen to pieces, while the Claytons of 1929, despite great neglect, were only just

The two CPR engines have never yet had permanent headlights fitted; the drill for night running, with any steam locomotive, is to rig a temporary battery-powered light. Here, at Hythe in 1973, its effectiveness as attached to *Winston Churchill* is demonstrated.

reaching that stage. Soundly built coaches made from high grade hardwood might cost half as much again compared with jerry-built ones, but the policy of jerry-building stood in ruins.

The policy of building short, low-capacity bodies on 16ft frames stood in ruins also. The cost of a new coachbody did not increase in proportion with its length or seating capacity, and as far as running gear was concerned, the considerable cost of renewal and annual maintenance varied hardly at all with the size of the coach. The standard 16ft frames had originally carried eight-seat bodies; their later postwar bodies with sliding doors had had 12 seats, but the extra four were 'kiddy' seats, rather inaccessibly located over the bogies and away from the doors, and it was not always possible to get people to use them, even when the train was full. For 25 years, the five 20-seat bodies on Eskdale frames had pointed the way; Howey had missed a trick when he had increased the length of the 1962 batch only sufficiently to accommodate 16, in 12 adult and 4 end seats. After consideration of the alternatives of going the next step up to a 24-seat coach, and of reducing the number of wheels by building

articulated sets again, it was decided to standardise on a 20-seat layout, using old 16ft frames lengthened to around 24ft with a new centre section. The paint shop which had been built in 1962 was extended and equipped to become a carriage building and maintenance shed, although for the sake of speed a number of new coaches were built by a contractor at Hythe. In addition, a number of new bodies were put on 20ft frames, both from the 1962 batch and from scrapped Clayton 'Pullman' coaches; lengthening these by a relatively small amount was not worth while. These vehicles included some guard's vans, with a six-seat compartment, luggage space, and a guard's seat fitted with brake valve and lookout windows.

Allchin was later succeeded as coachbuilder by Colin Bunn, who carried out the changeover from wooden to aluminium body construction after 1976, and who the following year built the most remarkable coach of all, the Bar Car. Ever since Heywood's time, the question whether a 15in gauge catering vehicle was really feasible had remained unanswered; he built one, but it really only seated children. There had been some fairly rudimentary experiments with selling drinks on the postwar saloons on the RH&DR, but not with success. It seemed time to try again. Producing some one-twelfth scale doodles around his office armchair as a basic seating module, the author finally schemed a seating layout at which a total of sixteen passengers could be accommodated on each side of a central bar with a double counter, behind which sat an attendant with sink, cooker, shelving, and storage. Drinks and light refreshments could be sold en route to passengers who had paid a small extra fare to travel in such luxury; gas heating and electric light are also provided. For several years, this vehicle was sponsored by Courage's Brewery and renamed the *Courage Belle*, thus doing both the railway and the brewers a good turn. In proportion to track gauge, at 32ft it is certainly the longest single unit railway vehicle in the world.

By building larger coaches it has over the years been possible to reduce the number on the books very considerably while more or less maintaining seating capacity. This also meant that sufficient vacuum brake equipment was available to fit almost every new vehicle, plus some of the old unfitted ones. Yet after nine years the renewal of the coaching fleet is still only half completed, and a considerable number of 8/12 seaters, though renovated, are still in service.

Perhaps the second most urgent problem in 1972 was the state of the buildings. Hardly a single structure was sound, well-roofed and watertight. This had been dramatised the previous summer when a customer fell through the floor of the Dungeness cafe; some ominous bulges in the rafters then directed attention to an

enormous 1500-gallon water tank in the attic which threatened to follow. The less said about any of the toilets the better. Hythe station was a deplorable shop window, and the roof of the engine shed was beginning to bang up and down in a high wind. All these matters needed attention. There was some doubt at first over the future of the Dungeness extension, but having studied the problem the new management came to the same conclusion as the old, that the railway's problems were not curable by amputation.

The situation on the locomotive front was not a whole lot better. *Samson* and *Southern Maid* had been soled and heeled, or given fairly extensive mechanical first aid, but some of the other machines were in a very poor way. In autumn 1971, at Bill McAlpine's request, *Doctor Syn* had been sent for a thorough overhaul to Cushing Engineering, at Rainham in North Kent. During the next few years, until Dick Cushing fell ill in summer 1978, he and his son also rebuilt *Hurricane* and *Typhoon*, plus a very radical reconstruction of *The Bug* (which Bill McAlpine had rescued from Belfast) and almost completed *Hercules*. Meanwhile Wingham Engineering, near Canterbury, overhauled *Winston Churchill* during 1974/75, and T.M.A. Engineering of Lichfield did *Northern Chief* in 1980/81. Because of the great amount of work needed on rolling stock and signalling, the New Romney shops for the time being left main overhauls of steam locomotives to these outside contractors.

One rare stroke of luck occurred in 1976. It was known that after Roland Martens had left Krauss of Munich, he had worked for the rival and

Snow is not common on Romney Marsh, but at times the school train must run through it. Here the Simplex, fitted with the Heywood plough ex-Eaton Railway, pilots *Winston Churchill* in December 1979.

The Bug rebuilt; Dick Cushing, rarely caught by a camera, on the footplate of the last engine he completed, leaving New Romney in 1978.

greater firm of Krupp which during 1937 built three 15in gauge Pacifics for an exhibition railway at Düsseldorf. These engines were recognisably derived from the Krauss design, but also included a number of features which Greenly and Martens had developed earlier for the Eskdale and Romney engines, among them the ineffective smokebox superheater. But the Krupps were robuster again than either, and more powerful. All three had survived the war, and had operated on a line in a park in Cologne. Following its closure in the mid-1960s, two had been acquired by Alan Bloom of Bressingham Gardens in Norfolk, but the third had disappeared from sight until the author received a letter out of the blue from a firm of fairground equipment dealers near Frankfurt, offering it and a quantity of rolling stock for sale. Inspection revealed that although slightly vandalised, the engine was basically in an ex works condition, and so it was purchased. Quite a lot had to be done to alter it to suit the RH&DR, including lowering the driver's position in the cab, fitting vacuum brakes, and replacing the original highly advanced Scharfenberg automatic couplers with Stephensonian buffers and hooks. But the net cost of the engine including all this was about the same as an outside contractor overhauling one of the original machines. A competition was run in a local newspaper to suggest a new name for it, the old one, *Fleissig Lieschen*, translatable as *Busy Lizzie*, being felt to be insufficiently dignified to conform with Romney standards. *Spitfire* was favoured by many; a good name for a steam locomotive anyhow, it would have made a useful Battle-of-Britain triplet with *Hurricane* and *Typhoon*, even though those were originally named after meteorological phenomena rather than aircraft. But in view of the Krupp's origins, this might have been a little tactless. By the balance of a hair it was decided to re-use the old name *Black Prince* instead.

Following the experience of their first season, the new management in autumn 1972 announced a plan for improvements to the railway. It was essential to improve the basic amenities first, and new lavatories at Hythe and New Romney, plus a new station building at Hythe, were soon under way. In Howey's day customers had had to queue in the rain outside a kind of overgrown sentry-box to buy tickets at Hythe; now there was an attractive entrance hall instead.

The largest single work was to start, at last, on rationalising the layout of New Romney station, making it simpler and therefore more economical to work. The key to this was the provision of a third through track and main platform. At the same time, a large overall roof was erected, partly to enable passengers to wait for trains under cover, but mainly to provide shelter for nearly all the coaches. Previously these had mostly to be kept, winter and summer, in the open air, with the result that decay was greatly accelerated. This roof has more than paid for itself in reducing carriage maintenance costs, although unfortunately it has not been possible to complete the scheme and modify its rather stark appearance with end gables.

Because of the improved working of this new station, and the construction of a passing loop on the Dungeness line at Maddieson's, it became possible in 1974 to introduce a revised timetable. More frequent trains, running at regular intervals, could be operated while still using the same number of sets of coaches. It was hoped that this would help attract more passengers; this happened to some extent, but with more trains going through to Dungeness there has also been some increase in average journey length, and with a more regular service some increase in the proportion of return journeys to singles. Both of these changes have been helpful.

Another change of policy since 1972 has been to concentrate track maintenance so far as possible on total relaying. At least one mile, sometimes nearly two, has been tackled each winter, using new timber sleepers (though steel ones were also tried). More ex-Sierra Leone rail was obtained, making a total of $2\frac{1}{2}$ miles of track, and this released a stock of re-usable original steel with which defective or corroded rails could be replaced. Total renewal in this manner, even using second-hand rail, is of course more expensive in the short term than patching and spot repairs, but much cheaper and more satisfactory ultimately. Only by using new timber could the desirable average annual rate of sleeper replacement be brought down to a tolerable level, and the only practical way to check the soundness of each rail is to lift it free of all fastenings and examine it closely, cutting off damaged ends when necessary and rejecting those with serious pitting or perforation from rust. Oddly enough this kind of corrosion is erratic; one rail can be reduced to something like lacework while others on each side are little affected.

All these things meant that over a few years there were immense changes to the appearance of the railway. But they were not achieved easily. Quite a lot of ill-luck dogged the enterprise; in particular, there were two deaths in 1973. Early that summer Richard North collapsed and died on the footplate of *Winston Churchill* in New Romney station; and on 6 August Peter Hobson, a member of the railway's staff as well as one of its

owning group, was killed while driving *Samson*, struck and derailed by a recklessly-driven stolen car at St Mary's Road level crossing. This wretched accident highlighted the problem of the unprotected level crossings, which had been only a minor nuisance in 1927, but which with the growth of road traffic were now serious. After discussions with the Ministry of Transport and the local authorities, all five crossings between Hythe and New Romney were fitted with automatic flashing-light warning signals, meeting the standard Ministry specification and designed and installed by the railway's own staff. Approximately half the cost of this work was paid by the local authorities.

Steady progress with physical rehabilitation was not, unfortunately, accompanied by much evidence of financial recovery. The Holding Company put a lot of money into these new works, but by 1976 it was clear that the supply of new shareholders willing to subscribe at least £1,000 without much prospect of any return was exhausted. The legal limit for a private company of 50 members was also about to be reached. On both counts it thus became imperative to 'go public' and attempt to raise a considerable amount of fresh capital by appealing to a wider body of shareholders, with a minimum investment reduced to only £100. The legal complexities of this process are quite horrendous and not to be faced by any small company unless desperation drives. At the same time and for other reasons, Sir Gerald Glover resigned as a director, W. H. McAlpine stepped down to become Vice-Chairman, and Viscount Garnock joined the Board as the new Chairman.

It was hoped to raise £250,000 by the share issue; unfortunately only about one third of this amount was ultimately found. Although this made it possible to pay off the load of debt incurred during the great spasms of rebuilding in 1973/4, it meant that the railway remained financially hamstrung, unable to complete a number of desirable improvements or indeed to see its way clear to any secure future.

Of course, things would have been all right if traffic had built up as had been hoped, but despite all efforts it never did. Instead of recovering towards the levels of the late 1940s, with over 400,000 passenger-journeys a year, it stayed around the 300,000 mark and indeed showed a tendency to decline further. Perhaps this was foreseeable, if the collapse of the Kent Coast as a holiday area had been taken into account. Over the last 30 years for example Folkestone, typically,

Black Prince the second; No 11 running into Hythe with a train consisting of the Bar Car and a rake of standard 20-seat teak saloons (and one teak open), 1980. (*P. H. Groom*)

has lost half its hotel beds. The old advantage of the area, its easy accessibility from London by rail (plus daily through trains from other parts of the country) no longer counted for much, nor did the through trains survive the electrification of the Dover and Folkestone main lines in 1960. Families now go on holiday by car, and the motorways from London run north and west, not south-east. There was also the boom in foreign holidays to consider.

One useful small item of business was won, with some publicity, in 1977 when the railway started to operate a school train daily throughout the year, bringing about 220 children from the Dymchurch area to school at New Romney. The circumstances were unusual, in that a large secondary school had grown up near the station, drawing many of its pupils from the ribbon of housing between the railway and the coast. The train terminated at Burmarsh Road, where the old station was reopened for it, and called also at Dymchurch and Jefferstone Lane. It was possible to win this business from contract buses because so many would have been needed; it was in fact an ideal trainload set-up, in the best Beeching manner. The load was heavy enough to need two locomotives in winter conditions, and until 1981 the standard operation was to have one at each end of the long set, which enabled it to be reversed at Burmarsh Road without any need for a loop or siding. The ideal, however, was a more powerful diesel locomotive at one end and a driving trailer coach at the other, and this was the pattern from 1981 using at first a machine borrowed from

Ravenglass, *Shelagh of Eskdale*. The school train brought in another 8–10 per cent of revenue; a useful boost, but hardly decisive.

The problem in fact was a simple one. The RH&DR is a world-famous jewel of its kind, but in a declining and unattractive setting. Tourism in the South-East has dwindled; traffic has gone the same way, for all the new team's efforts. The time must come when owners and management must take a stern decision; whether to sit tight and face a gloomy future, or to move to a new site with better potential before getting overwhelmed by debt. The RH&DR and its assets, its atmosphere, and its tradition, are worth keeping; but it cannot be kept unless it can earn its keep, and it could be kept elsewhere. The people of the RH&DR are determined to maintain the railway as a world-famous main line in miniature; and if it is not possible to do so on Romney Marsh, then on another and better site.

The Board came to this decision in early 1980, but also decided that it was its duty to put the matter to the local authorities in Kent to see if they wanted the railway to remain and were prepared to help it to do so. This caused a predictable political uproar; but during the following two years a series of meetings and exchanges of information persuaded the leaders of the local authorities that some help should and could be given. Exactly how much help, and whether it will be sufficient to secure the future, is still unclear at the time of writing.

The matter rests with local government simply because national policy has always ruled out any question of the RH&DR receiving any of the grants-in-aid that have been made to other independent, enthusiast-supported railways in other parts of Britain. This is not because of any judgment about their various merits, or about the local or national importance of tourism in their various areas, but simply due to a political decision taken for reasons having nothing to do with tourism, or railways, at all. During the 1970s some of these other railways, which are in a very real sense the RH&DR's competitors, began to receive donations of state funds which were very large in relation to their size, and which enabled them to buy new rail, new locomotives, new coaches, and even to build new lines, all in the name of the great sacred cow of regional policy that we have already noticed. These grants were, of course, intended nominally to relieve local unemployment caused by the decline of local industries, and the South-East, never having had much industry in modern times, was regarded as ineligible for this bounty. It may be doubted to what extent the problems of chronic unemployment can be relieved by encouraging steam railways, often largely operated by volunteer labour, to carry tourists through scenic areas never very close to the places where the dole queues exist, even if they seem close enough on the small-scale maps on the opposite walls of large comfortable offices in Whitehall. But the good fortune of these rival enterprises, and the glossy appearances some of them began to take on as a result of it, did nothing to encourage custom on the perhaps fundamentally sounder RH&DR. The devotion of central government to regional policy has however continued without abatement,

No 11 *Black Prince* leaving Hythe, 1979. (*P. H. Groom*)

whichever party is in power, leaving the Romney nowhere to turn but the local authorities, who are of course also, though not all of them realise it, fellow-sufferers under the same scourge.

While this book was in the typesetting stage the situation changed in two ways. First the local authority decided to assist the RH&DR by

Shovel action Romney style, demonstrated by Derek Walsh on *Black Prince*, 1979. (*Keystone Press*)

Shelagh of Eskdale, borrowed from the R&ER for 1982, approaching Hythe. This 4–6–4 diesel-hydraulic incorporates some framing and other parts from Heywood's 0–6–0T *Ella* of the Duffield Bank Railway (see p. 6). (*Paul Ross*)

funding a new diesel locomotive; secondly government grants for tourist attractions are now spread more evenly in most parts of the country.

There are perhaps four ways of looking at the RH&DR, and two of them seem very nearly contradictory, or at least involve looking through opposite ends of the same telescope. The first and probably the commonest way is to adopt the original Howey-Greenly point of view. On this, the railway is a main line in miniature, unique in the world; nobody anywhere else has ever attempted or achieved anything like it. It is a dreamland affair, a working-out in concrete terms of the vision which occurred to Count Louis Zborowski and the Grand Duke Dmitri in the shop in Holborn in 1918. It provides the joy of seeing a vast and vital human activity reduced to child scale, yet still functioning and alive; a finely-engineered mechanical equivalent of the craftsmanship in precious stones and metals of another Russian of that time, Carl Fabergé. This is the interpretation which the public, then and now, have favoured and which has drawn them back often and again over the years, father, son, and grandson. The modern nostalgia of steam power has been added to all this quite lately, and this is really quite different from the original vision, which was of something entirely up-to-date. Although the RH&DR is not by any means the only place where one may now go to see steam locomotives at work, since they are maintained in other reservations, it is one of the very few where they still work as hard and as fast as they used to on the main lines (and this includes much of the steam working which still does take place on some main lines; normally it is a rather pale shadow of what it was from the point of view of action, if not of polish).

Another way is to consider the RH&DR as a struggling small business, with all the usual modern problems of that class of undertaking, plus some of its own. This viewpoint is every bit as valid and interesting, and much more could be said about it than there is room for in this book. *Small is Beautiful* in more senses than one; the railway shares with other small independent entities the fact that its staff are basically doing what they want to do in preference to better-paid but less satisfying jobs elsewhere, while even now its management is relatively little involved in outside matters or irrelevant politics. But the idyllic side of this picture is not the only one. The railway's equipment has not yet been got into thoroughly good order, much expensive renewal is still needed, and it is still a strain on the pockets, and the patience, of its owners.

A third viewpoint is a more strictly economic one, to look at the contribution the railway makes to the economy of the district it runs through. There was a time when this could be very easily described. If a place had no railway, it suffered because it was cut off from cheap transport. If it had a line, or better still two, then it was in touch with the outside world. People could easily come and go, goods could be brought in more cheaply for sale, and local produce could be more readily delivered and so would fetch a better price. For this reason, it was very frequently worth while for the landowners and industrialists of a railless district to promote a local company which would bring the trains to them, even though they knew very well that it would have a hard struggle to survive and they stood a good chance of losing some or all of their investment in it. They would still have their reward indirectly, in the prosperity the line brought.

Things had just about stopped working like that, or being as simple as that, by the time the RH&DR was built. Sir Herbert Walker judged very accurately that the dying embers of public demand for a railway to be built across Romney Marsh were too far gone in 1926 to sustain an advance by the Southern company, which he was then conducting in the very last campaign of territorial expansion by any of the British main lines; the embers could just be fanned to sufficient heat for their purpose by Howey and Greenly. And without the public demand, not even Howey could have prevailed. By the mid-1920s it was already perfectly clear that road transport could meet the direct needs of movement of both goods and passengers in districts like Romney Marsh; all that has happened since then is that the balance of advantage has moved even further in favour of road. However, at the same time, public opinion had begun to grasp that a railway like the RH&DR could have another advantage to the locality it served, by bringing in visitors and attracting trade that way. It might perhaps be hard to put a strictly-calculated cash figure on this; but nobody who has seen the hundreds of thousands of happy people riding on the trains each summer can have much doubt that there was and is a real cash benefit to the district as a whole, and a substantial one, which continues into the 1980s.

The fourth viewpoint is the opposite of the first; you could say it is the view from the inside,

Doctor Syn on Half Mile Curve with a down train, 1980. (*P. H. Groom*)

looking out. Those who work on the railway, for instance, are not blind to the romantic vision of it, though it does not bulk very large with them. They are much more conscious of the human pleasure it brings to so many; they would have to be blind indeed not to see that. But a day-to-day, matter-of-fact, bread-and-butter approach has to be the overriding one. First must come the detail of the operation; the capacities and weaknesses of each piece of equipment, the problems of building, maintaining, and running it, in a thousand aspects, and above all the co-operation and teamwork needed to make it all go smoothly. This is the telescope-opposite of the romantic public view, but the last fulfils the first. How right and proper that somebody has to attack these dreamboat machines with spanners and muck-shovels; it proves they are alive.

In other words, one of the vital things about the railway is that it is possible, indeed necessary, to be completely matter-of-fact about it. It is a commercial undertaking, with some rather unusual machinery which has to be maintained and operated to perform a specific job efficiently. It has to earn enough income to pay its bills. In all this it differs not a whit from your friendly neighbourhood perambulator or baked-bean factory. Kipling wrote, '. . . yet all unseen, romance brings up the nine-fifteen.' He was right, of course; but hard slog does even more, as Kipling himself was also well aware.

So even if it started as One Man's Railway, the RH&DR had already ceased to be that by the time it first opened. It has a life of its own, as a child has. Some of the staff in the old days used to refer to Howey as 'Father'. Perhaps he was; but no parents ever own their offspring, when all is said and done.

Appendix

Telling the history of the Romney, Hythe & Dymchurch Railway has necessarily involved giving much technical detail. However, any history is a moving picture and must be fundamentally at odds with any attempt to give a clear description of the mechanical and organisational technicalities of any institution like a railway, which needs the equivalent of a set of still pictures. The purpose of this Appendix is to give this kind of description of the RH&DR as it exists at the beginning of the 1980s.

Staffing

Unlike some other preserved railways, the Romney is operated almost wholly by paid employees. They consist of a nucleus of around 25 permanent staff, working full time throughout the year. Those who drive locomotives in the running season do maintenance work in the winter, either in the workshops at New Romney or on the track; the same applies to several others with summer jobs such as booking clerk or signalman. Even so there are several people who do the same work all the year round, including a nucleus of skilled people in the machine shop, on carriage building and repair, and on buildings, model exhibition, and electrical maintenance. There is also the office staff, dealing with all kinds of work including accounts, advertising and promotion, planning and general administration, and so on.

Typhoon near Hoorne's Bridge in 1981, with a down train composed of the newest aluminium-bodied stock. The first three and last two vehicles are standard 20-seaters; between them is a six-seater plus guard and luggage van, and two opens. (*P. H. Groom*)

During the running season, except for a period in the spring when only a skeleton service is operated, the ranks of the regulars are swollen by seasonal staff; they are in general either students or pensioners, though not all the latter are necessarily over 65. At the peak, there are over 60 people on the payroll. The seasonal tend mainly to work at the various stations, and in the souvenir shops and cafes (including the Bar Car), but they cover also such tasks as carriage cleaners and travelling guards. This latter title is a rather odd Romneyism. On every other railway it is taken as a matter of course that the guard travels with the train, with or without a ticket-issuing machine and a bag of loose change. Even on the RH&DR there is in fact no guard who does not travel. But the job title is ancient, and so perhaps there did once exist a very rare species of guard who stayed in one place and was always left behind by the train.

Volunteer unpaid workers exist as well, and always have done. There are some regulars who come to the railway relatively frequently and do such jobs as guard or stationmaster or booking clerk; others come individually or in organised groups to carry out particular tasks of one sort or another, often centred on that fundamental and inescapable railway tool, the shovel. In early days the volunteers were perhaps slightly more gilded youths who generally drove, while most of the shovelling was done by the regulars; nowadays the position is rather the reverse, though without much gilding. It is policy to encourage the more useful young volunteers to become seasonal staff by paying them enough to be able to spend a longer time, perhaps a whole summer, on the railway.

The Romney, Hythe & Dymchurch Railway

Samson at Half Mile Curve in 1981, heading a down train composed of standard hardwood coaches of the 1973 design; the first is a six-seater plus guard and luggage van, the next a 20-seat open and the others 20-seat saloons. (*P. H. Groom*)

Association assists the railway in a number of ways including organising volunteers. One principle firmly established however is that the mere fact that a person has offered his services without pay does not give him any right to do as he pleases. Once his offer is accepted he must do as he is told; he is no longer a volunteer but a conscript. Those not liking this can take their services elsewhere.

Locomotive Running

This is perhaps the most glamorous of all departments on any steam railway, but a great deal of its work is not glamorous at all.

At the bottom and foundation of everything is the Firelighter, whose task it is to come in early every morning and raise steam in the engines scheduled for work that day. With the school train running throughout the year, and due to leave New Romney at 7.40 am, this means that every morning he must come to work in time to check the boilers, clear out the remains of the previous day's fires, and have the new ones burning on two grates before 6 am. During the high summer and in school holidays, the start does not have to be quite so early but even so he must raise steam similarly in anything up to six locomotives, starting before 7 am. All this must be done with total punctuality and dependability since everything else depends on it. Other than steam-raising, and chopping up old sleepers for

firewood, the Firelighter is a general handyman around the shed, much of whose remaining time is spent carrying out variations on the theme of shovelling. It is laborious, dirty and unpublicised work, but responsible and vital, partly because of the need for punctuality and also because ignorance and carelessness could cause serious damage.

The driver, on the other hand, is prominently in the public eye, though his job is no sinecure either. On the RH&DR, except in winter when normally only three engines are kept serviceable for working the school train, each regular driver normally keeps to his own locomotive, and this gives him the chance to fix many little items as he wishes, as well as giving him added incentive to clean and polish it. The extra cost of having the engine idle when he has a day off is not great, but money well spent under the circumstances, particularly considering that Captain Howey made the capital investment required in the palmy 1920s. When he comes to work each morning during the running season, he finds his engine with steam up and has an hour or so to prepare it for the day's work, including oiling round, heaving three or four hundredweight of coal into the tender, and various other small jobs such as adding the right amount of boiler treatment chemicals to the water in the tender. On the run he is on his own on the footplate, unless he has a trainee or occasionally an authorised passenger. His day is long, and although some days he may be lucky enough to work a 'gentleman's turn' of only 45 miles (twice to Hythe and once to Dungeness) his duty is more likely to be 62 or 73 miles (three times to Hythe and once or twice to Dungeness). Plenty of standard-gauge locomotive crews cover less distance in a day's work on a BR diesel, for much more money. All the time he must keep an eye open for signs of trouble with his engine or his train, including heated bearings, broken springs, anything on the line, and so on; he is on his own throughout, except that there is somebody else to push the turntable round for him at Hythe and New Romney. In fine weather he can at times relax on the run and enjoy the breeze; in heavy rain he may shelter under a canvas stormsheet which he can rig between tender and cab roof; high winds can at times blow the coal off his shovel on exposed sections of line before he can put it on the fire.

At the end of the day he must clean out the smokebox, sweep the tubes, withdraw the woollen wicks which feed oil into the various pipes which take it where it is needed (so they don't siphon oil all night over the shed floor) and having made sure the boiler is full of water and the damper closed so the fire will die, he can go home after what is usually about a 12-hour day during the summer. This is in fact very heavy work. Normally during the peak he can expect to work for six days consecutively, then have one day off and one shed day when apart from any minor repairs or adjustments, his main job is to wash out the boiler of his engine, removing a week's accumulated sediment. This involves taking out several screwed washout plugs from the boiler, which have to be put back carefully and not cross-threaded, or else they are apt to blow out with something like the force of a small anti-tank gun; they have then of course to be checked when steam is next raised. One has to be pretty devoted to it to put up with the labour of a job like this; the compensation is in having control of a marvellously responsive and fascinating machine. It was a perceptive person who first called it an Iron Horse.

In the past, and particularly during the peak traffic years of the late 1940s, daily mileages much greater than the 62 or 73 of today were achieved quite often. In those days many trains were run extra or as required, and not shown in the published timetable, while nowadays such workings are relatively few. Most of the extra runs were Hythe to Dymchurch shuttles, with one or sometimes two engines and sets of coaches going rapidly to and fro on the five-mile section, the locomotive using the then two crossovers at Dymchurch to run round and returning tender-first. Making seven, eight, or more such journeys in a day, together with the dead-head running from and back to New Romney, daily mileages of

over 90 and sometimes over 100 were quite common. But drivers did not then, as they do now, have to put away their engines at the end of the day, including tube cleaning.

Bob Hobbs, who joined the staff in 1946 and drove *Hercules* during the post-war years, has kept the notebooks in which he recorded in detail every day's work. He ran a large number of the ballast trains, having worked the first post-war one with his engine on Thursday, 28 November 1946. This conveyed 24 loaded wagons, which was about normal; the heaviest load he records was on 11 September 1947 when he took 35 loaded wagons from the Ballast Siding to Hythe in little over the usual 80 minutes, despite the train breaking in two. But then Howey did not like seeing his engines overloaded, or even working hard.

Generally the ballast train was a late shift job, leaving the pit about 4.30pm. Unlike most passenger workings, it was double-manned, with driver and guard, the latter riding on the little four-wheeled brake truck obtained from the Eaton Railway. On arrival at Hythe the loaded wagons had to be winched two by two up the ramp and tipped into the various hoppers, which might take anything from two to four hours. The return workings to the Ballast Sidings with the empties thus usually got back at about midnight or 1am, and with the engine still to put away at New Romney, time off duty was about an hour later still.

Normally at Hythe the driver operated the incline winch, which was powered by a small electric motor, and the guard rode a wagon up the ramp to tip the loads. Once the inevitable happened and the rope broke; the wagons roared off down the incline at an amazing speed, guard hanging on for dear life, and came to rest just short of the Prince of Wales Bridge. The guard had had his coat and shirt ripped off his back by bushes and brambles as he flashed past, but fortunately nothing worse.

In the peak holiday season the ballast engine had to do some passenger work as well. One long day was Monday, 7 July 1947, when Hobbs came on duty at 8.30am and started with the 9.30 regular train to Hythe, loaded to 16 coaches. Its return working to New Romney was extended that day to Maddieson's Camp, but because of the crowds at New Romney, even though the train was made up to 23 coaches, two return journeys had to be made to the Camp. There followed two more 16-coach workings to Hythe and one return to New Romney; on arrival at Hythe at 4.30pm

Hobbs had his first break for a cup of tea before setting off light engine at 5.18 for New Romney. There was then time for a sandwich or two before going on to the Ballast Sidings to start the day's work rather later than usual, 6.48pm. With the normal goods running time of 80 minutes each way from the Sidings to Hythe, and three hours working the ramp, return to shed was at 1.05am, not much later than normal. The total day's work had spanned $17\frac{1}{4}$ hours from signing-on to signing-off, and covered 86 miles.

Another variation occurred on Tuesday, 18 August 1947. On that day Hobbs booked on at 1.30pm to stand by with his engine, but in fact was not required for any passenger work that afternoon. An attempt was therefore made to get the ballast job through a bit earlier than usual, and he set off with engine and brake van from New Romney for the Ballast Sidings at 4.42pm, where a train of 26 loaded wagons was waiting. But on returning he was held at New Romney for signals from 5.31 to 5.38, and was then spiked firmly at Dymchurch, being ordered into the siding from 5.54 to 7.22pm to free the line for passenger trains and wait until Hythe station was sufficiently clear to give access to the ramp. Fortunately unloading took only two hours that night, and leaving Hythe with the empties at 10.40 for a smart run back to the Sidings, arriving at 11.50, they were back at New Romney at 12.25am for the normal 1am finish.

Sometimes one train a day was not enough to clear the ballast traffic, and when this happened a second engine would be sent out. During the running season, this extra freight had to be timed to get to Hythe after the regular one was clear (with both drivers warned not to attempt to pass each other on the Willop Bridge). This usually meant reaching Hythe around midnight, and a departure with the empties between 2 and 3am. On these very late workings, the empties were generally left at New Romney to be taken on next morning, so that the driver could get home an hour or so earlier, and ahead of the milkman.

To cater for all this night running, there were experiments with headlights. *Hercules* ran for a time fitted with one large spotlight mounted on the bufferbeam, powered by a small reciprocating steam-driven generator set adapted from one of the 'jungle-burner' outfits intended for use behind the Japanese lines in the 1944/45 Burma campaign. This was not a very powerful set, being intended only to power a portable radio transmitter, and so it had to be supplemented with a rank of batteries. All this equipment was removed when the Hythe ballast working ceased, and the amount of night running declined.

The sad thing about all this effort was that it made no money for the railway. Howey charged the ballast company 1d (less than $\frac{1}{2}$p) per ton-mile for hauling the shingle, because that was the traditional main-line mineral rate. On such a short haul a much higher charge would have been justified, and still been well below the cost of road transport. Drivers' wages on the RH&DR in 1947 were 2s per hour for the basic 44-hour week, but only 1s 10d per hour for overtime (has any other railway ever paid less per hour for overtime than for the main part of the day?) A 24-ton train on the 10-mile haul to Hythe would thus earn exactly £1, not nearly enough to cover the driver's wages let alone the guard, the coal burnt, or any of the other costs. Still, it was arguably only a paper transaction; at the time Howey was the principal shareholder in the ballast company as well as owner of the railway.

Boiler treatment is an important matter on RH&DR locomotives. Some steam railways are fortunate enough to run in an area with soft water, which contains little dissolved matter and where a locomotive boiler can run for weeks before needing to be cleaned out. On the other hand, most soft water is slightly acid, and therefore tends to corrode away the metals inside the boiler, particularly when following normal British (but not RH&DR) practice, the combination of a copper firebox and steel tubes and barrel sets up an electrolytic action as well, with the boiler acting as a large and permanently short-circuited battery. Water in the Romney Marsh area is quite hard, with a lot of dissolved lime and chalk which tends to form hard scaly deposits on firebox and tubes. If these are allowed to build up they will prevent heat passing into the water and ultimately cause the steel to be damaged by local overheating. If suitable chemicals are added to the water, this hard scale can be converted into a soft sludge which is easily removed, and other chemicals can at the same time reduce corrosion, but these additives all increase the total amount of dissolved matter in the boiler water and make frequent washing-out imperative. Five or six days is quite long enough between washouts, although blowing some of the sludge out daily under pressure through a suitable blowdown valve is a modern, ie post-1930, method of lengthening this period. Until the 1950s, the RH&DR used no water treatment, and suffered accordingly; tube life was around 6–7 years and at 30 years boilers and fireboxes began to need renewal. Since that time, close attention has been given to proper water treatment; tube life is now a very comfortable 15–16 years, and the postwar boilers, some of which are now nearly as old as those they replaced, still in very good condition.

During the winter, some drivers move onto permanent way work and some to maintenance of brakes and running gear on the passenger coaches; the remainder, apart from continuing to work the winter period trains, are employed on annual locomotive (and rolling stock) maintenance. As a rule the engines need little machine shop work. The main item is preparing each boiler for annual inspection, with all plugs, grate, and ashpan removed; the tender also has to be cleaned out and the coal space checked for corrosion (coal rots steel quite quickly), and various minor repairs done on each machine. About every 10 or 12 years, each locomotive becomes due for a heavy overhaul, during which it is completely dismantled and rebuilt with all bearings, axleboxes, slides, pins, etc, renewed or renovated. At the same time, the wheels will all be turned to the correct tread profile on a lathe; most engines are now within sight of their third set of new driving wheel and bogie tyres, or have already received them.

Miniature Locomotive design

The RH&DR is probably not unique in having, after half a century, all 10 of its original locomotives still on the property and in service, though the record must be pretty unusual. *The Bug* admittedly had 20 years submerged in a scrapheap in Belfast, and now contains only a limited amount of its original metal; it also belongs now not to the railway company but to Bill McAlpine. But all the same, there it is at New Romney and from time to time it comes out to work a train.

Records of individual locomotive mileages before 1946 no longer exist, but it seems clear that each machine, except perhaps the 4–8–2s, must have run at least 300,000 miles and probably considerably more in a number of cases. The earlier Pacifics, which did most of the pre-war work, may have run upwards of 400,000 miles each. On average each is capable of running about 75,000 miles between heavy repairs, which was a respectable figure for a full-size main-line locomotive of their period. Although driving-wheel diameter was a dimension much agonised over by locomotive designers in the nineteenth

century and railway enthusiasts in the twentieth, experience has shown that the 4–6–2s with their $25\frac{1}{2}$in diameter wheels and the 4–8–2s with theirs of $19\frac{1}{2}$in diameter are capable of the same work. If anything, the 4–8–2s are faster over the road, having better acceleration and the same practical maximum speed, which in any case depends on the limit set by track rather than rpm or piston speed. They do however tend to put up rather lower mileages between repairs, due simply to increased wear and tear. As always, there is absolutely no black magic about it. But with these quite impressive records, it is clear that Greenly and Paxman made a pretty good job of them originally, and there is not a lot wrong.

All the same, there are certain weaknesses which could be put right with a new machine or a rebuilt one. Past improvements have included superheating, and fitting most engines with bigger and better tenders. Nothing can be done, feasibly, on the existing engines about the inadequate clearance between frames and driving wheels, for instance, which often leads to the frame plates being quite severely cut into by the flanges and prevents the adoption of a more modern tyre profile which would reduce maintenance by extending mileage between wheel-turnings (this is being done with coaching stock). The leading bogie on every engine is of the same poor design, and somewhat troublesome to maintain. Perhaps something can be done some time about the poor weight distribution, too heavy at the firebox end, too light at the front. This is always a tendency with miniature locomotives, and results in an increased likelihood of slipping. The two CPR engines have never looked quite right (not surprising considering their history), most noticeably because the chimney top lies below the level of the cab roof. Perhaps some day their looks will be improved with longer copper-capped chimneys, in the style of Baldwin *circa* 1900. They really ought to have proper electric headlights and perhaps turbo-generators. All the engines could benefit from the more normal modern refinements like roller bearings, which did so much to extend mileage between shoppings in the last 30 years or so of steam development.

Black Prince, as the odd man out, provides an interesting comparison. More powerful and heavier than the original machines, it was nevertheless designed by somebody who had studied Greenly's ideas closely, and even repeated some of his mistakes; for instance, the absurd grid-type smokebox superheater, removal of which instantly produced a dramatic reduction in coal and water consumption. Before 1982 only a minimum of work had been done to 'Romneyise' it, mainly connected with getting the driver down with his head below the level of the cab roof, so that it was not knocked off going under bridges, and also to allow it to accept standard spare parts like injectors, water gauge glasses, and Clupet-type piston and valve rings. Some further improvements, together with completion of the conversion of the braking system from Westinghouse to vacuum, were undertaken when the engine received a general repair in 1982.

The main secret of the success of the steam locomotives is just that they are amply solid and robust. Most miniature locomotives, steam or diesel, fail because their designers do not appreciate the need to make everything at least three times stronger and heavier than on any other kind of moving machine, if it is to stand up to commercial service. A good example of this is provided by the fleet of three small four-wheeled internal-combustion machines used for works trains and shunting. Most senior of them is the ex-Eaton Simplex, built like a tank and in fact to a design which dates back to the military railways of the first world war. There are no refinements; the two-cylinder diesel motor now fitted has to be started by hand; no lights, no vacuum brake, no synchromesh. But it reliably potters away and will pull, slowly, any load coupled to it. In contrast, the two motorcar-engined petrol-powered units, though faster, are always in trouble because their components are simply not robust enough for railway service, and the maintenance staff long for the day of their withdrawal. But their speed, self-starting ability, and headlights, combined with an adequate haulage capacity for track inspection and repair work, make them operationally indispensable. One is a remote descendant of the old War Department light locomotive which was built in 1933 for the Sound Mirror construction gang and the branch line from Maddieson's Camp. Though re-bodied, re-framed, re-engined, re-gearboxed, and re-designed more than once, it still incorporates the original reversing axle and had, until 1982, its original wheels. The other originated on a private railway in a garden in Birmingham, belonging to Louis Jacot, and has also been much rebuilt. It now incorporates automatic transmission, separate reversing gearbox, and chain drive to all wheels, though using chains much less robust than those of the Simplex.

As and when circumstances allow, there is certainly a need for a heavy-duty diesel locomotive of about 100 horsepower, capable of working passenger trains, with all the refinements but also built like a battleship (or a steam locomotive). The school train obviously makes a strong case for this machine, but it would be very useful in ordinary service as well. A lot of work has been done to develop such a design, and the experience gained from the visit of the Eskdale's *Lady Wakefield* in 1980, which was also based on these principles, was most valuable. In 1981/2 the other main line diesel from Ravenglass, *Shelagh of Eskdale*, spent a year at New Romney on loan in exchange for *Black Prince*.

Rolling Stock construction and design

An outline of the development of RH&DR passenger coaches has been given in the body of the book. Having started with four-wheelers of the kind adequate for small garden-party 15in gauge lines like the Sand Hutton, the need for something more robust, comfortable, and smoother-riding was discovered at once, and most of the original vehicles were replaced within 10 years. It followed from this that the RH&DR, as the only railway of its kind in the world, had to establish its own design requirements.

One was for a degree of all-weather comfort; another for this to be given within the confines set by track gauge and bridge clearance. The overbridges originally allowed coaches 6ft high to pass; this was reduced in the mid-1930s by 6in, to avoid drainage problems at New Romney, and stock had to be cut down in height, a brutal operation. The third requirement was for minimal maintenance, and a large step towards this goal was taken in the 1930s with the adoption of roller bearings as standard. The major difficulty was in allowing comfortable seating within the height restriction, and the answer was to carry the floor of the coach as low as possible, in a well between the wheels and only a few inches clear of the rails. This meant that the bogies had to be fitted underneath the end seats, not possible without some waste of (length-)space. In the lavish Clayton 'Pullmans' this otherwise useless volume was available for luggage, with four extra doors per coach giving access to two tiny end compartments. In the Hythe saloons of the 1930s it was just wasted space, boxed in and left. Since the war the tendency has been to fit seats above the bogies, regardless of restricted headroom; children can easily use them, and adults often manage to follow.

The comfort of the best pre-war coaches has been mentioned. The author can well remember how impressive it was, soft seats with plenty of leg room, much superior to the old boneshaker-type SR stock of which then there was still plenty about, even on the main line to London in the late 1940s. Not even the best recent RH&DR coaches have reached these levels of comfort again, let alone steam heating; economics dictate otherwise. However they are perhaps more substantial.

On a level line, brake adjustment is needed fairly infrequently and in general RH&DR coaches need no attention to running gear between their annual examinations in the winter months. The solid cast steel wheels last about 30 years on average, requiring to be taken out for re-profiling five or six times during their lives. New harder wheels with a more modern tread profile should last longer than this, with less re-profiling required.

The carriage numbering system sometimes excites remark; it seems odd that a railway with only 60 or 70 coaches should have some of them numbered in the low 800s. But there is a certain method to it, consisting of allotting blocks of numbers to different types of coach, and underframe. Some types no longer exist, and others have been added; but the scheme, based on the one instituted by the army during the war, is as follows:

Number Series	Coach Type
1–100	Saloon bodies on standard frames of Hudson type
1–33	Saloons on original 16ft Hudson frames (8–12 seats)
51–	Post-1972 Saloons on Hudson frames extended to 24ft (20 seats)
77	Bar Car, built on Hudson frame lengthened to 32st (16 seats)
100	Platelayers' Mess Coach on frame extended to 24ft (11 seats)
101+	Coaches using original Clayton 'Pullman' 20ft frames, with non-standard Gibbins bogies
101–105	Post-1972 rebuilds: luggage/guard/6-seat brake vans (105 also fitted as Driving Trailer)
110–117	Original 12-seat Clayton 'Pullman', now all dismantled except No 110 (not in service)
141–142	Post-1972 16-seat opens
201+	Works and freight equipment (see below)
300+	Ex-Eskdale 6-ton ballast wagons, rebuilt with 20-seat coach bodies
400+	Open-sided 16-seat built on standard 16ft Hudson frames (only post-1972 bodies now remaining)
451–	Post-1972 20 seat opens on extended 24ft Hudson frames
500+	Bogie luggage vans on standard Hudson frames (type now extinct)
600+	Semi-open 12-seat coaches (windows, no doors) on 16ft Hudson frames (type now extinct)
698–699	Ex-Eaton Railway Heywood stock (now returned to Eaton Hall)
700+	Four-wheeled passenger coaches or Guards Vans (types now extinct)
800–807	Saloons on 20ft Gower frames of 1962 batch (16 seats)

Except for the 101+ series, all vehicles can be fitted with bogies of standard type, either Hudson or Gibbins interchangeably, though the 300+ series originally had heavy-duty Gibbins freight bogies. Some vehicles have the suffix P after their number, denoting that they have no operating vacuum brake but are merely piped to enable them to run in vacuum-fitted trains. The ex-Eaton passenger coaches, surviving examples of which have now been returned to Eaton Hall, were radically different, with timber frames; two of semi-open type had their special place in the numbering system but the other two were simply numbered as they fell in the 400 and 500 series.

Saloons and brake vans built since 1978 have been fitted with electric light powered from batteries in the van; 77 and 100 are warmed by catalytic propane gas heaters. Maybe one day steam heat will reappear – perhaps.

There are in addition 48 works and freight vehicles, ranging from bogie flat wagons and a tool truck to four-wheeled skips, flats, and frames carrying a concrete mixer, a rail bender, and diesel-powered generator and compressor.

Track

The original track was laid with ex-military rail, either American 25 lb/yard, or the closely similar Belgian 12kg/metre, on new treated softwood sleepers, fastened with rather small spikes (3in × ⅜in). Howey used to say that it was laid with staggered joints, (ie with one joint opposite the mid-point of the other rail) because his experience in Canada had convinced him that this method gave a smoother ride than conventional European opposite-jointed track. While he may have said this, the fact remains that there was really no consistency on the RH&DR at all. In places, particularly leaving New Romney for Hythe, the original track was in fact opposite-jointed; but joints actually fell quite at random, sometimes accurately staggered but often with one leading the other by only 1–2ft, and anything in between. What seems to have happened is that the second-hand rails contained a fair number of random short lengths, down to as little as 6 or 7ft long; instead of being scrapped, or instead of cutting the inside rail shorter going round a curve, rails were simply laid down as they were unloaded and came to hand, for the sake of economy. With the track in good order and well maintained, this did not really matter; once things started to slip, and labour to be curtailed, this track became extremely rough as railjoints began to drop. The great majority of rails were however of a standard length of 30ft.

Sleepers have always been closer spaced than on standard gauge, averaging just under 2ft between centres. This was certainly helpful, considering the very poor ballast, a mixture of shingle, sand, and ash, often with clay an inch or so below the sleepers. Replacement sleepers obtained from British Railways were of slightly larger cross-section than the originals and so tended to remain more firmly fixed in the ballast, which was also helpful. But two further developments by the 1950s had advanced track deterioration even further. One was corrosion of rails; the other was the fact that as the original undersized spikes lost their grip in the decaying sleepers, rails started to move or creep along in the direction of traffic. On the single Dungeness line, this effect was not felt, but on the double track it became quite serious. In some places rails were moving by as much as 2ft a year; the resulting stresses caused the track to buckle in hot weather where the rails had piled up in compression, while in cold weather bolts and even fishplates would snap where they were in tension. The rails would then instantly spring apart by anything up to 2–3ft. Fortunately this always happened on cold nights with the first frosts, rather than when trains were running.

First aid repairs to these 'open joints' or defective rails involved putting in replacement rails without troubling always to ensure that they were of the same type; or filling a gap with a short piece perhaps only a few inches or a foot or so long. Both these sorts of repair produced additional bangs and lurches, but no follow-up permanent repairs were normally done. By 1972, when the situation was at last taken in hand, some sections of track had become appallingly rough and were putting up the cost of maintenance even

further by breaking springs. A year's effort resulted in the removal of well over a hundred 'janglers', short lengths of rail a few inches long, suspended by a lash-up of bolts and fishplates, from the track between Hythe and New Romney.

Post-1972 policy has been where possible to use new timber sleepers, either jarrah (durable Australian hardwood, needing no treatment) or treated Douglas Fir, or experimentally steel, depending on price.

Staggered- or irregular-jointed track is being steadily eliminated. Experience, on Romney Marsh as in North America, has demonstrated that this pattern needs much more maintenance to keep in trim and once deterioration sets in the effects are much worse. The dipping of alternate railjoints is apt to set up an alarming and sometimes dangerous rolling, exactly as one might expect.

The original American rail on the RH&DR is now approaching the end of its economic life, and since it comprises about two thirds of the total rail in use in 1980 this means the RH&DR now faces an expensive problem. The Belgian rail is still in reasonably good order and fit for many years to come.

Signalling and Operating

The method of working the double line, by telephone block, based on a standard army method and also used on certain BR freight lines, is described on page 69. No other method has been used. The post-war single line has also always been worked very simply, by the staff and ticket method, described on page 65. No need has ever been felt for any more complex or expensive methods of safe working, though if some of the existing double track is singled this might not still apply.

Passenger lines in the station areas at Hythe and New Romney are controlled from signalboxes at these two stations, which operate the points and signals through mechanical interlocking. Formerly all the signals were traditional semaphores; Howey replaced all these with colour-lights during the 1950s, partly to keep up-to-date, and partly because they were cheaper. Two semaphores were however reinstated mainly for sentiment at Hythe in 1975 to control departures; since both are adjacent to the signalbox little mechanical aggravation is involved.

All five level crossings with public roads on the double track section are now equipped with standard automatic flashing-light warning signals, operated from track circuits. When the road signals have been detected as operating correctly, a white flashing light is displayed to the train driver, and if he does not see this he must stop before reaching the road. Special arrangements ensure that if a second train is approaching the road while the first is crossing, the road signals will remain in operation unless there would be at least 10 seconds clear before they would re-start. At Dymchurch station, because of the closeness of level crossings at each end of the platforms, rather different arrangements apply and the semi-automatic three-aspect railway signals here are electrically interlocked with the road signals so that no green aspect can show unless the road signals are proved to be working, and this arrangement replaces the white flashing light. Semi-automatic here means that these rail signals are cleared manually, but restore themselves to danger when a train passes.

Strategic control of operations is maintained by an official at New Romney, who supervises the telephone block and makes all decisions on changes to plans, addition of extra coaches to strengthen certain trains for booked parties or for sudden rushes of business, and so on. It helps considerably, of course, that this can be done very quickly with 15in gauge equipment.

Train Services and Timetabling

The RH&DR's layout is considerably more complex than any other private steam railway in Britain, and this, coupled with the fact that the depot and headquarters are at a mid-point rather than at one end of the line, make its operations equally complex.

One starting point in designing the timetable is to decide how many locomotives will be required to work it. No driver can reasonably be given more than a certain amount of work to do, and the time during which he is to do it should not be too long drawn out. However unless his duty is a short one he should be given a break of about an hour during the day, which will mean another engine taking over his train at New Romney. A normal turn of duty involves three return trips to Hythe and one, or exceptionally two, to Dungeness; each extra engine brought out should thus be given this amount of work. The number required to be steamed each day varies from one to six depending on the level of traffic; allowing for the additional complexities brought in by the school train, this involves eight or nine different working timetables, each of which will have different times of engine-changing at New Romney and different patterns of coach working.

The railway has paid dearly over the years for the original mistake in placing the depot at New Romney instead of Hythe. Visualising the line as an extension of the SR New Romney branch was of course the reason, but that has been closed for many years and even before it went, Hythe was always the more important source of traffic. In effect each engine's first and last trip each day is an empty stock working to or from Hythe, and between 15 and 20 per cent of total annual train mileage is commercial waste. But experience has shown that having one or two engines based at Hythe, where there is a small engine shed, solves nothing; the only solution would be to move the whole depot, engineering and all.

Express or non-stop trains have often been a feature, particularly as Howey loved driving them himself. They may not have been so easy to justify in strict commercial terms. A daily scheduled non-stop run the whole length of the line was introduced after the war and given various names at various times: The Bluecoaster, The Coronation Limited, The Marshlander, and so on. By the mid-1950s the train had ceased to be non-stop, and after Howey's death it no longer carried a name, since it was found that this tended to concentrate passengers inconveniently onto the one working. A daily non-stop run was however reintroduced in 1977, the railway's Golden Jubilee year, with (naturally) The Golden Jubilee. However in commercial terms the cost caused by the disruption of orderly working by this train, which involved, for instance, maintaining one set of coaches to do no more than one trip a day from New Romney to Hythe and back, filling in a gap in the regular-interval service while the Jubilee was zooming down to Dungeness, was by no means justified by its rather poor loadings. Since 1979 the Golden Jubilee has therefore been cut down to Saturdays only; this is rather a quiet day with fewer trains scheduled and one spare set of coaches anyhow. This avoids the utilisation problem, while diehard steam enthusiasts tend to be more numerous on Saturdays anyhow. With only 42 minutes allowed for the $13\frac{3}{4}$ miles, this train re-creates more of the atmosphere of fast main-line steam running in the old days than can often be found elsewhere. It is all part of the atmosphere and character which makes the RH&DR unique. One Man's Railway it might have been but it is now up to us all to keep it that way.

systems operate like tramways without any signalling, except on single-track sections. Several continental systems are equipped with means of operating traffic lights themselves in urban areas; for instance an LRT vehicle approaching a cross-road can from some distance away, operate with its pantograph the traffic lights in its favour before it arrives at the cross-road.

Compared with 80 passengers as the carrying capacity of the latest and largest double-deck bus, the capacity of an LRT eight-axle-articulated vehicle is 250 or more and the new Tyneside six-axle-articulated vehicle can carry 208 passengers. LRT vehicles are, of course, single-deck cars with a minimum of seats while the standing-room is quite capacious. For example the Tyneside vehicles carry 84 seated and 124 standing passengers with the result that seats are available for all passengers at off-peak periods and at peak times the standing capacity can be fully utilised. Moreover two six-axle units normally run in pairs so that 400 passengers can be carried. Comparing specific examples, to move 8000 passengers an hour would need 100 80-seat double-deck buses or 32 LRT units of 250 passenger capacity, the latter on roughly a 2min headway. But LRT services can run at frequences of 1min or less so that 20,000 passengers an hour is quite feasible, but totally impracticable for buses.

The maintenance of a high commercial speed on public transport routes is particularly important for both operator and passenger. The higher the speed the fewer are the vehicles and staff needed and the more attractive is the service for the customer; 200 to 250 passengers on high-capacity vehicles with *only one operator* require a much higher degree of off-vehicle ticket sales than is normal in Britain. The most efficient European undertakings have eliminated cash handling on the vehicle by 98 per cent though the use of agencies or ticket-machines which are being installed at all the main stops. As tickets which are purchased from the driver usually cost 50 per cent more there is a minimum delay at stops. All tickets have to be cancelled by the passenger at cancelling machines distributed throughout the cars. There are penalties, payable on the spot, for not cancelling a ticket or over-riding, enforced by travelling inspectors.

Being of much lighter construction than normal heavy rail vehicles, acceleration and deceleration are most impressive and a speed of 80km/h (50mph) on segregated sections is easily attained.

In addition to the new extensive Tyne & Wear LRT system formally opened by the Queen in 1981, which has attracted more passengers than was either anticipated or estimated in forward planning, feasibility studies have been undertaken for LRT systems, in places integrated with existing and disused rail systems and in Birmingham and Manchester they are in the stage of forward planning. The London Dockland LRT project is now under construction.

While Tyne & Wear is an entirely segregated LRT system, it has possibilities for some street operation, and Birmingham's 'Rapid Transit for The West Midlands' will exploit and upgrade some lines on the British Rail network, in addition to constructing a new Rapid Transit lines which could share the streets with other vehicles in some places and be segregated in others.

Two of the new Tyne & Wear LRT six-axle-articulated units coupled together passing over the Byker viaduct constructed to carry the new line over the Ouseburn Valley. This structure won the prestigious 1980 Concrete Society Award and also won a commendation from the Royal Fine Arts Commission. (*Tyne & Wear PTE*)

British Electric Tramways Undertakings: Opening and Closing Dates

MUNICIPALLY OWNED

Town	Gauge ft	in	Opening–Closing Dates
Aberdare	3	6	1913–1935
Aberdeen	4	8½	1899–1958
Accrington	4	0	1907–1932
Ashton-under-Lyne	4	8½	1902–1938
Ayr	4	8½	1901–1931
Barking	4	8½	1903–1929
Barrow	4	0	1904–1932
Batley	4	8½	1903–1932
Belfast	4	8½	1905–1954
Bexley	4	8½	1903–1935
Birkenhead	4	8½	1901–1937
Birmingham	3	6	1904–1953
Blackburn	4	0	1899–1949
Blackpool (including Fleetwood)	4	8½	1885–still operating
Bolton	4	8½	1900–1947
Bournemouth	3	6	1902–1936
Bradford	4	0	1898–1950
Brighton	3	6	1901–1939
Burnley	4	0	1901–1935
Burton-on-Trent	3	6	1903–1929
Bury	4	8½	1903–1949
Cardiff	4	8½	1902–1950
Chester	3	6	1903–1930
Chesterfield	4	8½	1904–1927
Colchester	3	6	1904–1929
Colne	4	0	1903–1934
Coventry	3	6	1895–1940
Croydon	4	8½	1901–1951
Darlington	3	6	1904–1926
Dartford	4	8½	1906–1935
Darwen	4	0	1900–1946
Derby	4	0	1904–1934
Doncaster	4	8½	1902–1935
Dover	3	6	1897–1936
Dundee	4	8½	1900–1956
East Ham	4	8½	1901–1940
Edinburgh	4	8½	1922–1956
Erith	4	8½	1905–1935
Exeter	3	6	1905–1931
Glasgow	4	7¾	1898–1962
Gloucester	3	6	1904–1933
Grimsby	4	8½	1901–1937
Halifax	3	6	1898–1939
Huddersfield	4	7¾	1901–1940
Hull	4	8½	1899–1945
Ilford	4	8½	1903–1938
Ilkeston	3	6	1903–1931
Ipswich	3	6	1903–1926
Keighley	4	0	1904–1924
Kilmarnock	4	8½	1904–1926
Kirkcaldy	3	6	1903–1931
Lancaster	4	8½	1903–1930
Leeds	4	8½	1897–1959
Leicester	4	8½	1904–1949
Leith	4	8½	1905–1920*
Leyton	4	8½	1906–1939
Lincoln	4	8½	1905–1929
Liverpool	4	8½	1898–1957
London	4	8½	1903–1952
Lowestoft	3	6	1903–1931
Luton	4	8½	1908–1932
Lytham St Annes	4	8½	1903–1937
Maidstone	3	6	1904–1930
Manchester	4	8½	1901–1949
Middlesbrough	3	6	1898–1934
Nelson	4	0	1903–1934
Newcastle-on-Tyne	4	8½	1901–1950
Newport	4	8½	1903–1937
Northampton	3	6	1904–1934
Nottingham	4	8½	1901–1936
Oldham	4	8½	1900–1946
Perth	3	6	1905–1929
Plymouth	3	6	1899–1945
Pontypridd	3	6	1905–1931
Portsmouth	4	7¾	1901–1936
Preston	4	8½	1904–1935
Rawtenstall	4	0	1909–1932
Reading	4	0	1903–1939
Rochdale	4	8½	1902–1932
Rotherham	4	8½	1903–1949
Salford	4	8½	1901–1947
Sheffield	4	8½	1899–1960
St Helens	4	8½	1900–1936
Southampton	4	8½	1900–1949
Southend	3	6	1901–1942
Southport	4	8½	1900–1934
South Shields	4	8½	1906–1946
Stockport	4	8½	1901–1951
Stockton	3	6	1898–1931
Sunderland	4	8½	1900–1954
Swindon	3	6	1904–1929
Wallasey	4	8½	1902–1933
Walsall	3	6	1902–1933
Walthamstow	4	8½	1905–1939
Warrington	4	8½	1902–1935
West Ham	4	8½	1904–1940
West Hartlepool	3	6	1896–1927
Wigan	3 6 / 4 8½		1901–1931
Wolverhampton	3	6	1902–1928
Yarmouth	3	6	1902–1933
York	3	6	1910–1935

* Taken over by Edinburgh at this date

COMPANY OWNED

Town	Gauge ft	in	Opening–Closing Dates	Town	Gauge ft	in	Opening–Closing Dates
Aberdeen Suburban	4	8½	1904–1927	Stalybridge	4	8½	1904–1945
Airdrie & Coatbridge	4	7¾	1904–1956	Sunderland District	4	8½	1905–1925
Barnsley	4	8½	1902–1930	Swansea	4	8½	1900–1937
Bath	4	8½	1904–1939	Swansea & Mumbles	4	8½	1929–1960
Bessbrook & Newry	3	0	1885–1948	Taunton	3	6	1901–1921
Birmingham & Midland	3	6	1904–1930	Torquay	3	6	1907–1934
Bristol	4	8½	1895–1941	Tynemouth	3	6	1901–1931
Burton & Ashby	3	6	1906–1927	Tyneside	4	8½	1902–1930
Camborne & Redruth	3	6	1902–1927	Wemyss & District	3	6	1906–1932
Carlisle	3	6	1900–1931	Weston-super-Mare	4	8½	1902–1937
Chatham & District	3	6	1902–1930	Wolverhampton District	3	6	1900–1928
Cheltenham & District	3	6	1901–1930	Worcester	3	6	1904–1928
Cork Electric Tramway	2	11½	1898–1931	Wrexham & District	3	6	1903–1927
Cruden Bay	3	6	1899–1932	Yorkshire (West Riding)	4	8½	1904–1932
Dearne District	4	8½	1924–1933	Yorkshire Woollen District	4	8½	1903–1934
Dewsbury & Ossett	4	8½	1908–1933				
Douglas Southern Electric	4	8½	1896–1939				
Dublin United Tramway Co	5	3	1896–1949				
Dudley & Stourbridge	3	6	1899–1930				
Dumbarton	4	7¾	1907–1928				
Dundee, Broughty Ferry	4	8½	1905–1931				
Dunfermline	3	6	1909–1937				
Falkirk	4	0	1905–1936				
Gateshead	4	8½	1901–1951				
Giant's Causeway	3	0	1883–1949				
Glossop	4	8½	1903–1927				
Gosport & Fareham	4	7¾	1906–1929				
Gravesend & Northfleet	4	8½	1901–1929				
Great Crosby	4	8½	1900–1925				
Great Grimsby	4	8½	1901–1937				
Greenock & Port Glasgow	4	7¾	1901–1929				
Grimsby & Immingham	4	8½	1912–1961				
Guernsey	4	8½	1892–1934				
Hastings	3	6	1905–1929				
Hill of Howth	5	3	1901–1959				
Isle of Thanet	3	6	1901–1937				
Jarrow	4	8½	1906–1929				
Kidderminster & Stourport	3	6	1898–1929				
Lanarkshire Tr Co	4	7¾	1903–1931				
Leamington & Warwick	3	6	1905–1930				
Llandudno & Colwyn Bay	3	6	1907–1956				
Llanelly & District	4	8½	1911–1933				
London United Tramways	4	8½	1901–1936				
Mansfield District	4	8½	1905–1932				
Manx Electric	3	0	1893–still operating				
Merthyr	3	6	1901–1939				
Metropolitan Electric	4	8½	1904–1939				
Mexborough & Swinton	4	8½	1907–1929				
Middleton (Lancs)	4	8½	1902–1935				
Musselburgh & District	4	8½	1904–1954				
Norwich	3	6	1900–1935				
Notts & Derbyshire	4	8½	1913–1932				
Paisley & District	4	7¾	1904–1957				
Peterborough	3	6	1903–1930				
Portsdown & Horndean	4	7¾	1903–1935				
Potteries	4	0	1899–1928				
Rhondda	3	6	1908–1934				
Rothesay	3	6	1902–1936				
Scarborough	3	6	1904–1931				
Sheerness	3	6	1903–1917				
Snaefell Mountain	3	6	1895–still operating				
South Lancs Tramway Co	4	8½	1903–1933				
South Metropolitan	4	8½	1906–1937				
South Staffordshire	3	6	1893–1930				

In a few systems with a departure from the more usual 3ft 6in, 4ft and 4ft 8½in gauges, it will be noticed that the peculiar gauge of 4ft 7¾in was adopted (notably in the Clyde Valley area). This was to enable railway wagons to be run on the tramway tracks. The depth of the flange of a railway wagon is greater than the depth of the groove of a tram rail and so the railway wagons had to run on the flanges of their wheels instead of on their tyres, the taper of the flanges necessitating a reduction of tramway gauge of ¾in. Some commercial firms in Glasgow owned their own electric locomotives for hauling railway wagons loaded with coal and other materials between their works and railway sidings over the tramway tracks by arrangement with the tramway undertaking.

The foregoing table of British electric tramway undertakings gives the names of the towns initially operating electric tramways or the dates they electrified their previous horse or steam tramways. In some cases the identity of the original operators had been changed by its being merged or absorbed; in these cases the closure date indicates the demise of the original electric tramway undertakings.

In Ashton-under-Lyne, Barrow in Furness, Birmingham, Colne, Coventry, Devonport, Grimsby, Lytham St Annes, Middlesbrough, Poole, Shipley, Southport, Stockton, St Helens, Walsall and West Hartlepool electric tramcars were introduced and operated by companies before being taken over by the municipal authorities; also in some cases municipalities owned the lines in their areas allowing them to be operated by companies.

Bibliography

Anderson, R. C. *A History of the Midland Red* (David & Charles)

Jackson-Stevens, E. *British Electric Tramways* (David & Charles)

'Kennington' *London County Council Tramways Handbook* (Tramway & Light Railway Society)

Lawson, P. W. *Birmingham Corporation Rolling Stock* (Birmingham Transport Historical Group)

Palmer, G. S. and Turner, B. R. *Blackpool by Tram* (published by the authors)

Taplin, M. R., and others *Light Rail Transit Today* (Light Rail Transit Association)

Webb, J. S. *Black Country Tramways Volumes I and II* (published by the author)

Willoughby, D. W. & Oakley, E. R. *London Transport Tramways Handbook* (published by the authors)

Index

Belfast Corporation Tramway, 53
Birmingham Corporation Tramways, 53, 55
Black Country Electric Tramway systems, 57, 58, 61, 62
Bradford Tramways, 36
Bristol Tramways & Carriage Co Ltd, 37
British Electric Traction Co Ltd, 14, 34, 35, 61, 62

Cable Tramways, 7, 50
Cheap Fares on electric tramways, 32, 48, 56
Competition from:
  motor buses, 47, 73–76
  private cars, 85
Contrast with thriving continental systems, 86–88
Crescent rail, 8
Croydon Tramways, 35

Destination indicators, 28
Double-deck tramcars, 19, 42
Dudley Corporation, 62
Dundee Tramways, 34

Economic advantages of electric tramways, 16
Edinburgh Tramways, 50
Electric tramcar equipment, 19, 20, 21

Feltham type tramcars, 45, 46, 50

First British street electric tramway, 8
First electric tramway, 8

Gauges and Opening & Closing dates of British electric tramways, 94, 95
Glasgow tramways, 55, 56, 68

Halifax Tramways, 36
Huddersfield Tramways, 36

Inauguration of first British street electric tramway, 8
Installation of tramway electrical equipment, 16
Isle of Man system, 70

Leasing problems, 33, 35, 36
Leeds Corporation Tramways, 50, 67
Light Rail Transit (LRT), 90–93
Liverpool Corporation Tramway, 51, 53
Local Authorities:
  difficulties with, 13, 14
  oppressive powers of, 14
London County Council:
  conduit track, 15, 34, 41
  inaugural electric tramcar, 41
London's various tramway systems, 37, 40, 41
London United Electric Tramways, 37

Manchester area tramways, 36, 48, 57
Metropolitan Electric Tramways, 37

Metropolitan police authority, 42

Newcastle-upon-Tyne tramways, 92, 93

Overloading of tramcars, 63

Passenger carrying capacity comparisons, 93
Pioneer of first British electric street tramway, 8
Platforms of electric tramcars, 27
Preserved electric tramcars, 88–90

Segregated tramway tracks, 64–68, 70, 72
Sheffield Corporation Tramways, 48
Special tramcars, use of, 32
Steam tramway locomotive, 6
Stud contact system of current collection, 15
Swansea & Mumbles Railway, 68

Taunton electric tramway, 48
Tramcar liveries and coachwork, 24, 25
Tramways Act 1870, 8
Tramway water tank cars, 15
Types of tramcars in initial stages of electrification, 22

Wartime difficulties, 76, 77, 79, 80
Workmen's fares, 32
Wolverhampton stud-contact current collection system, 63